The Art Of Mandala

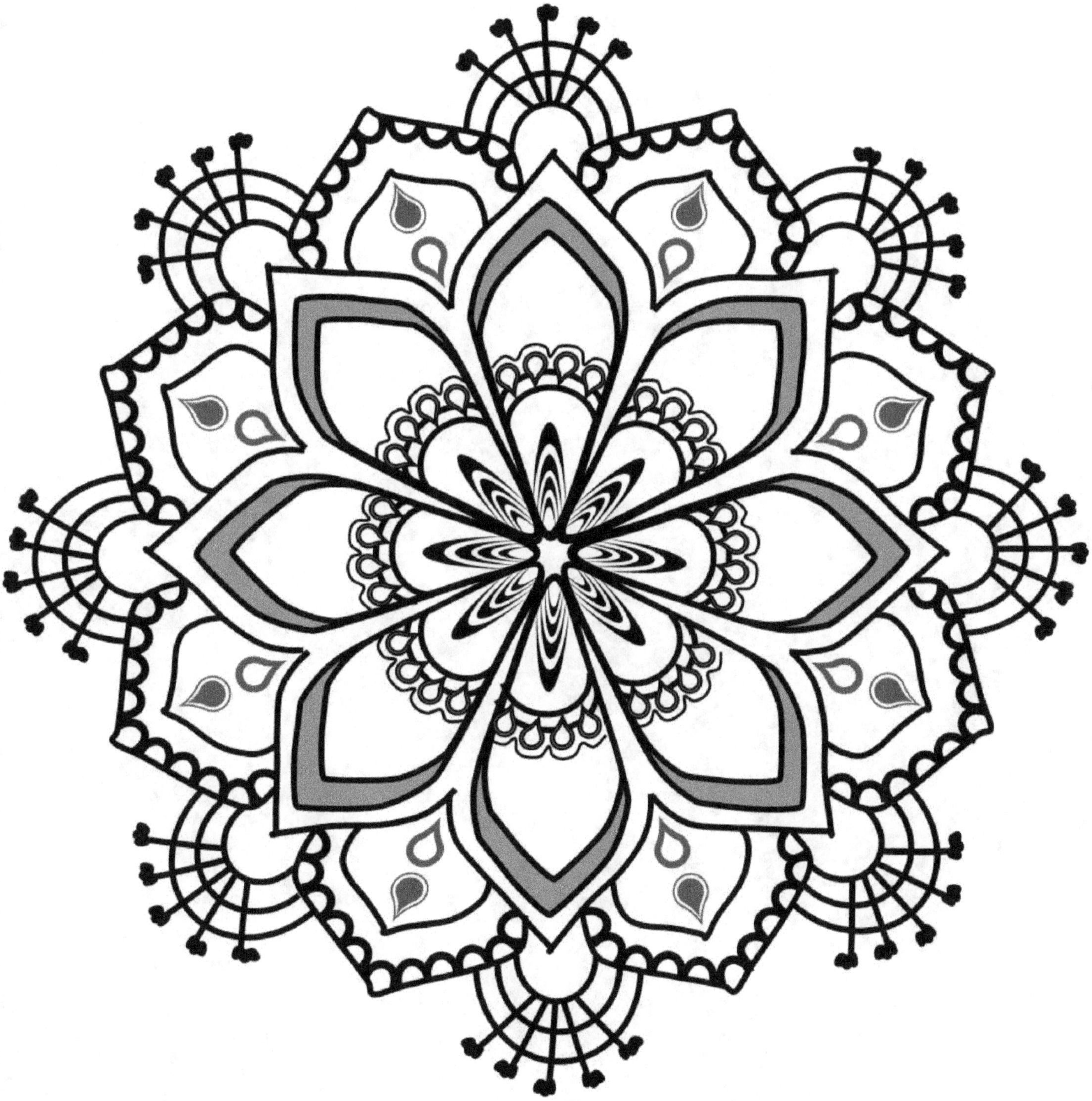

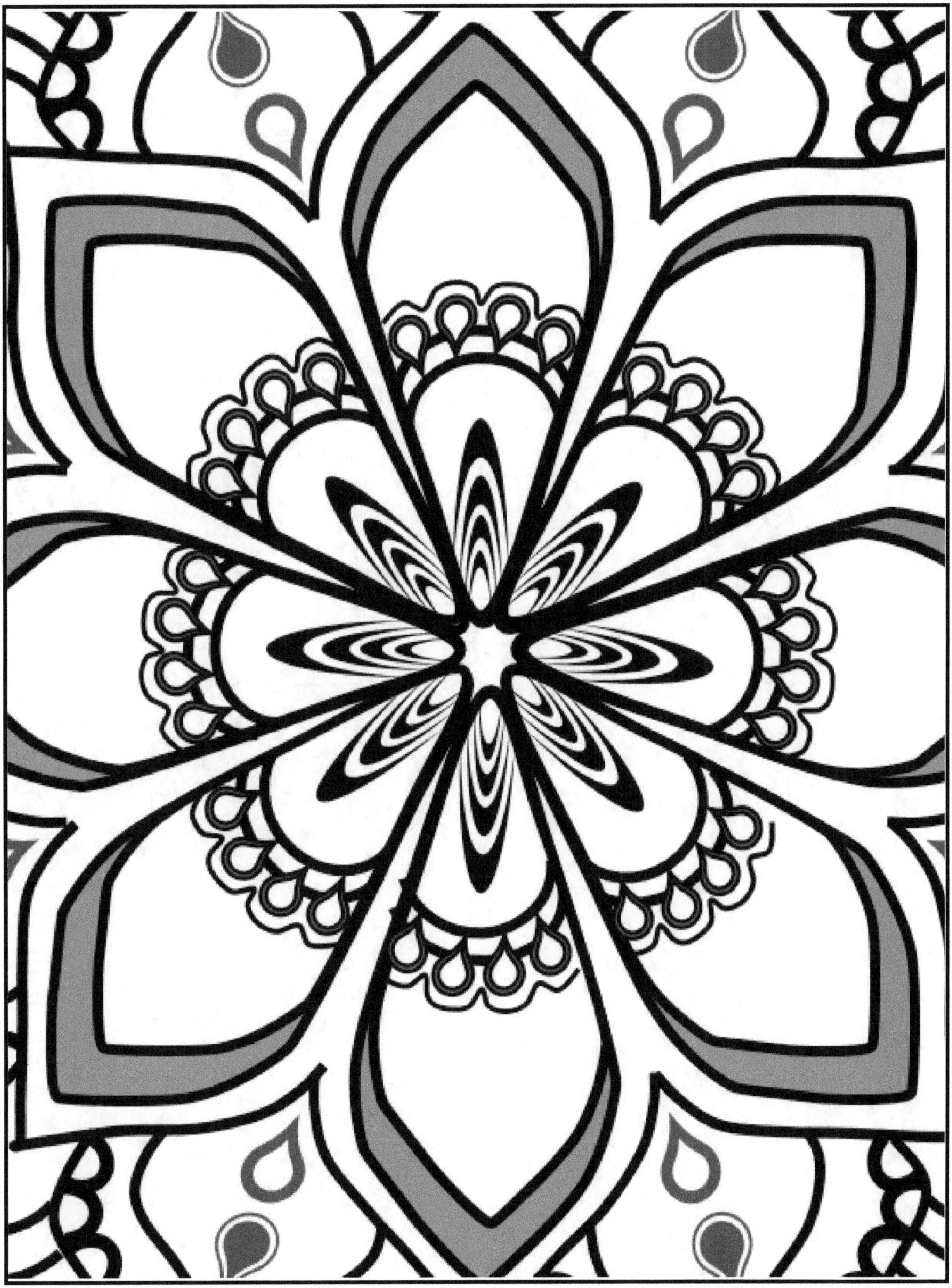

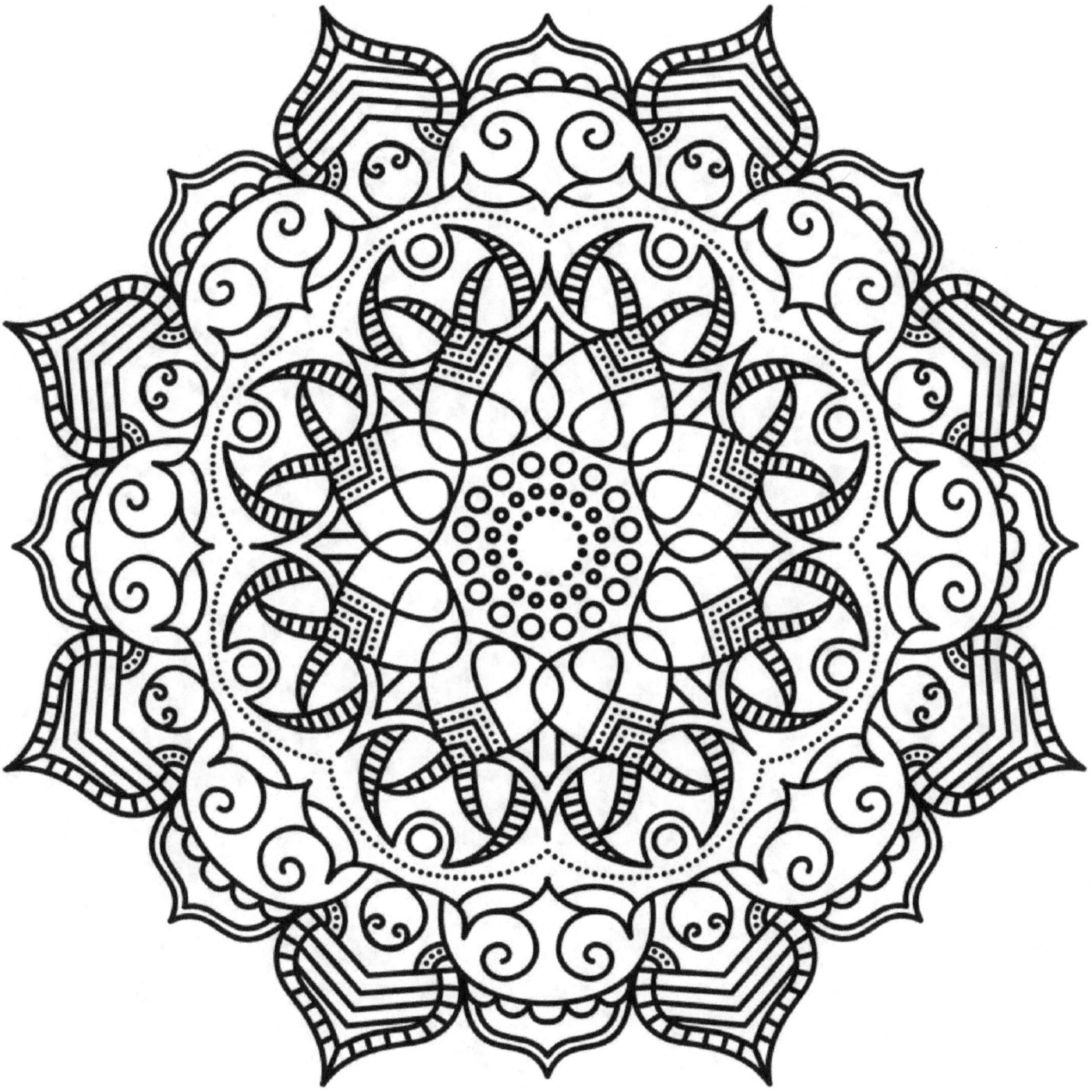

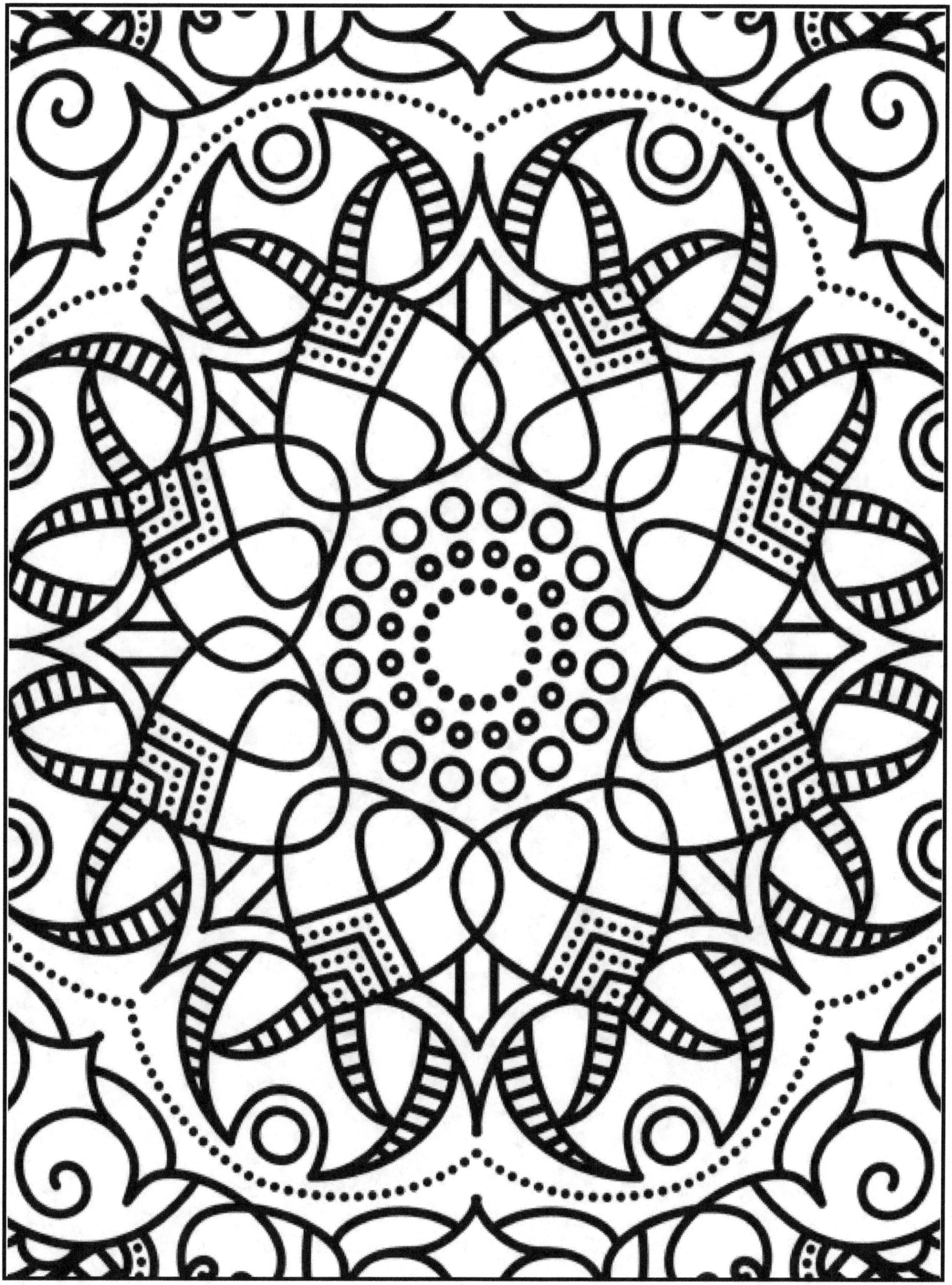

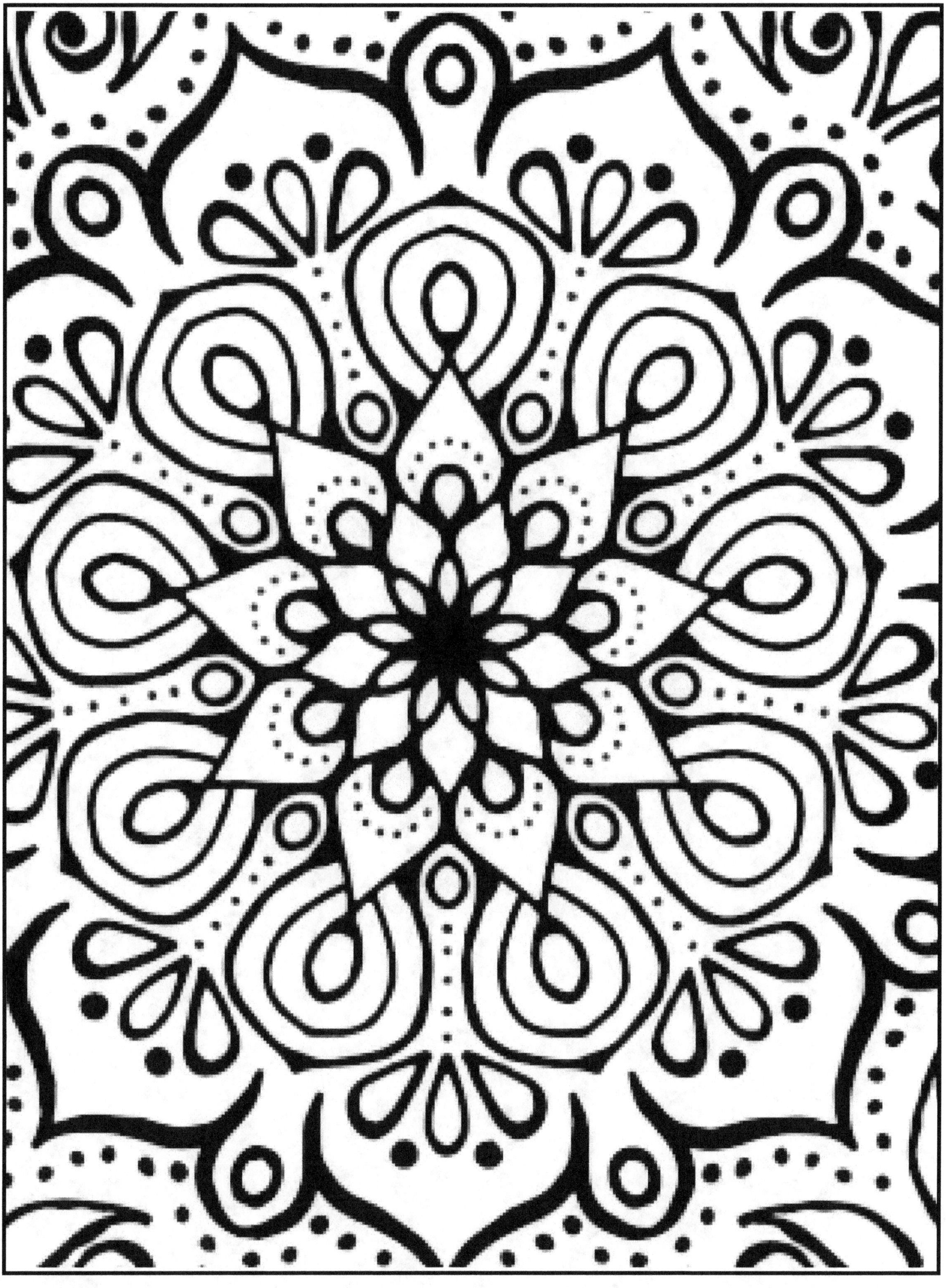

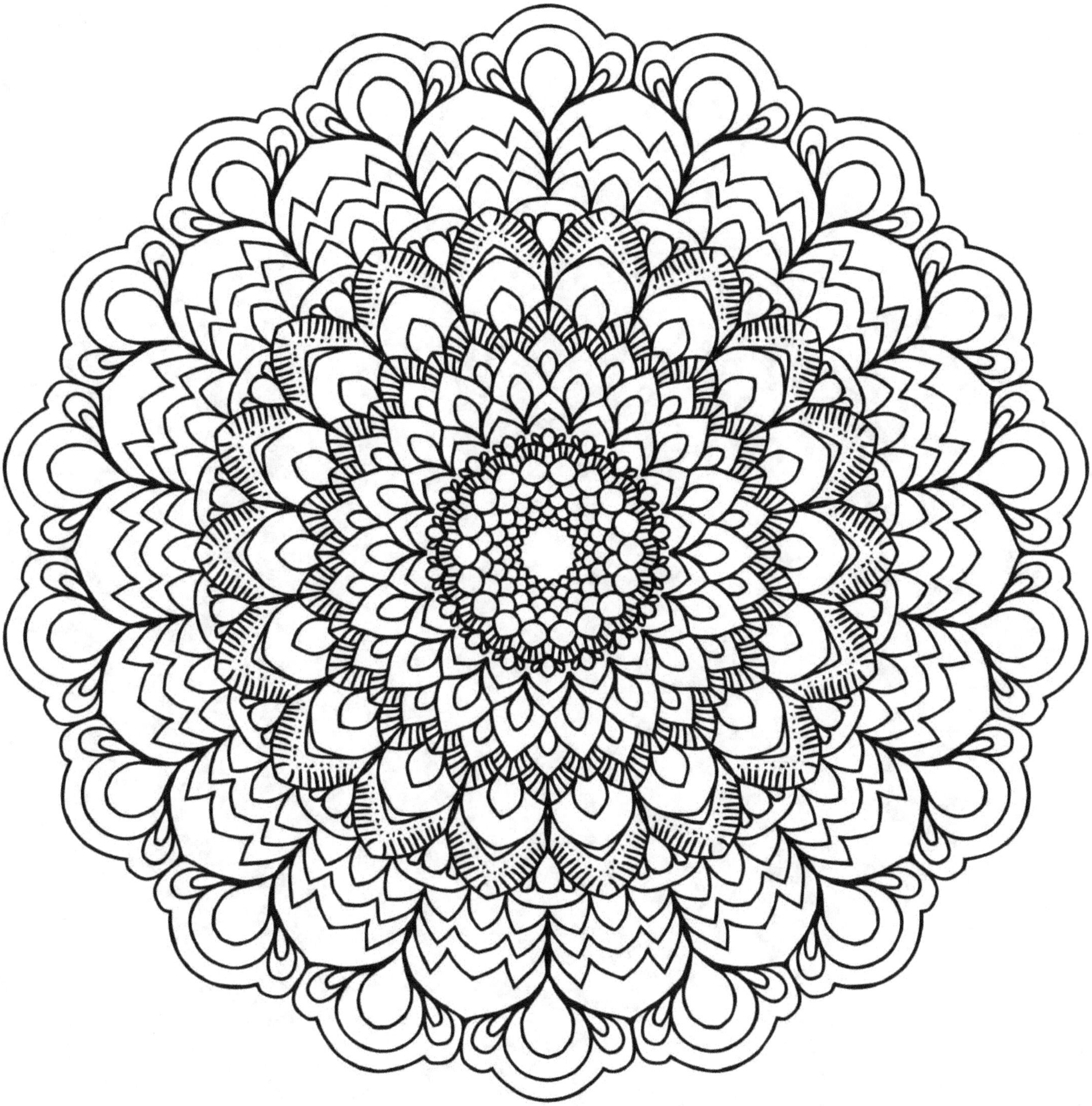

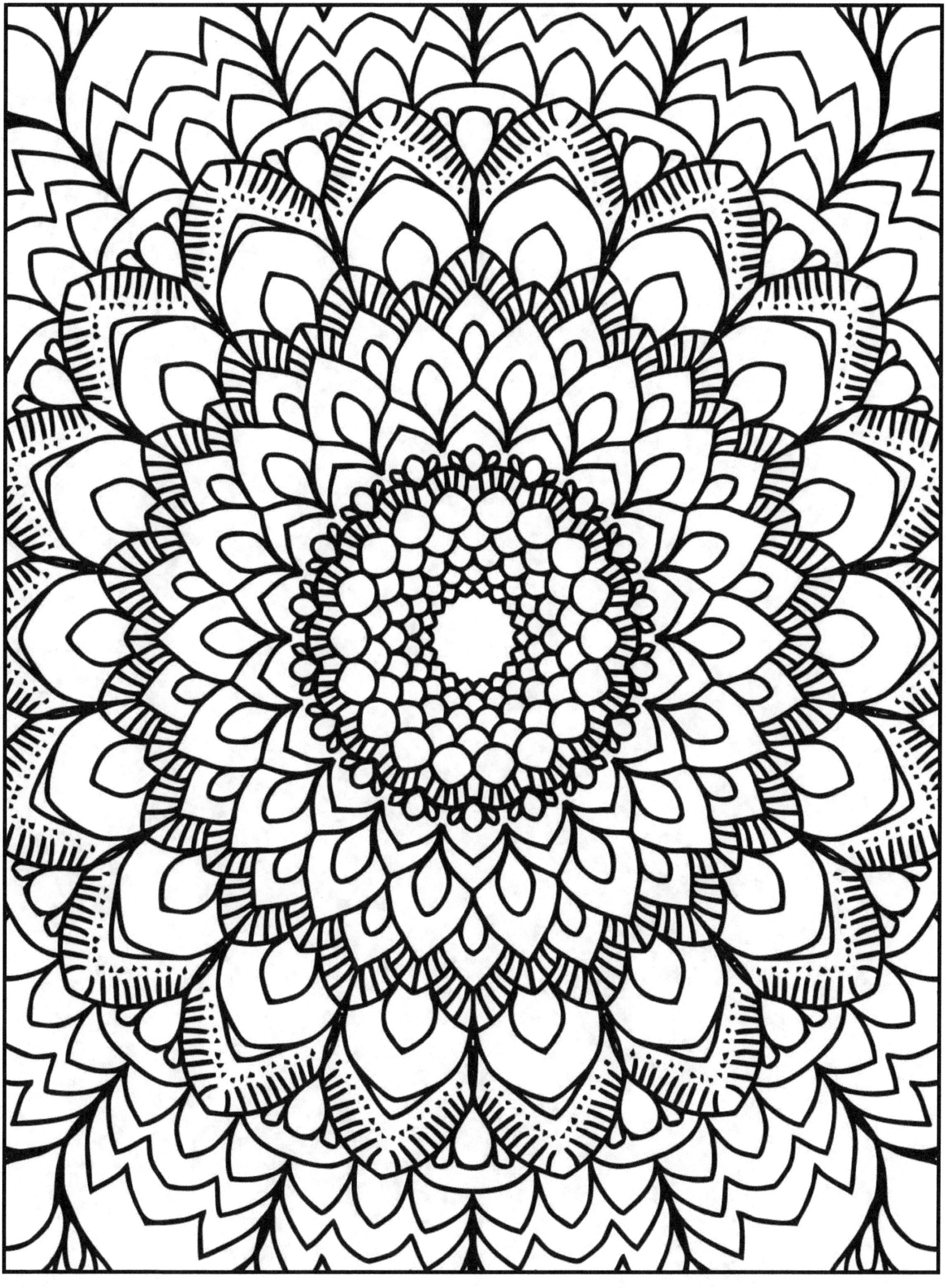

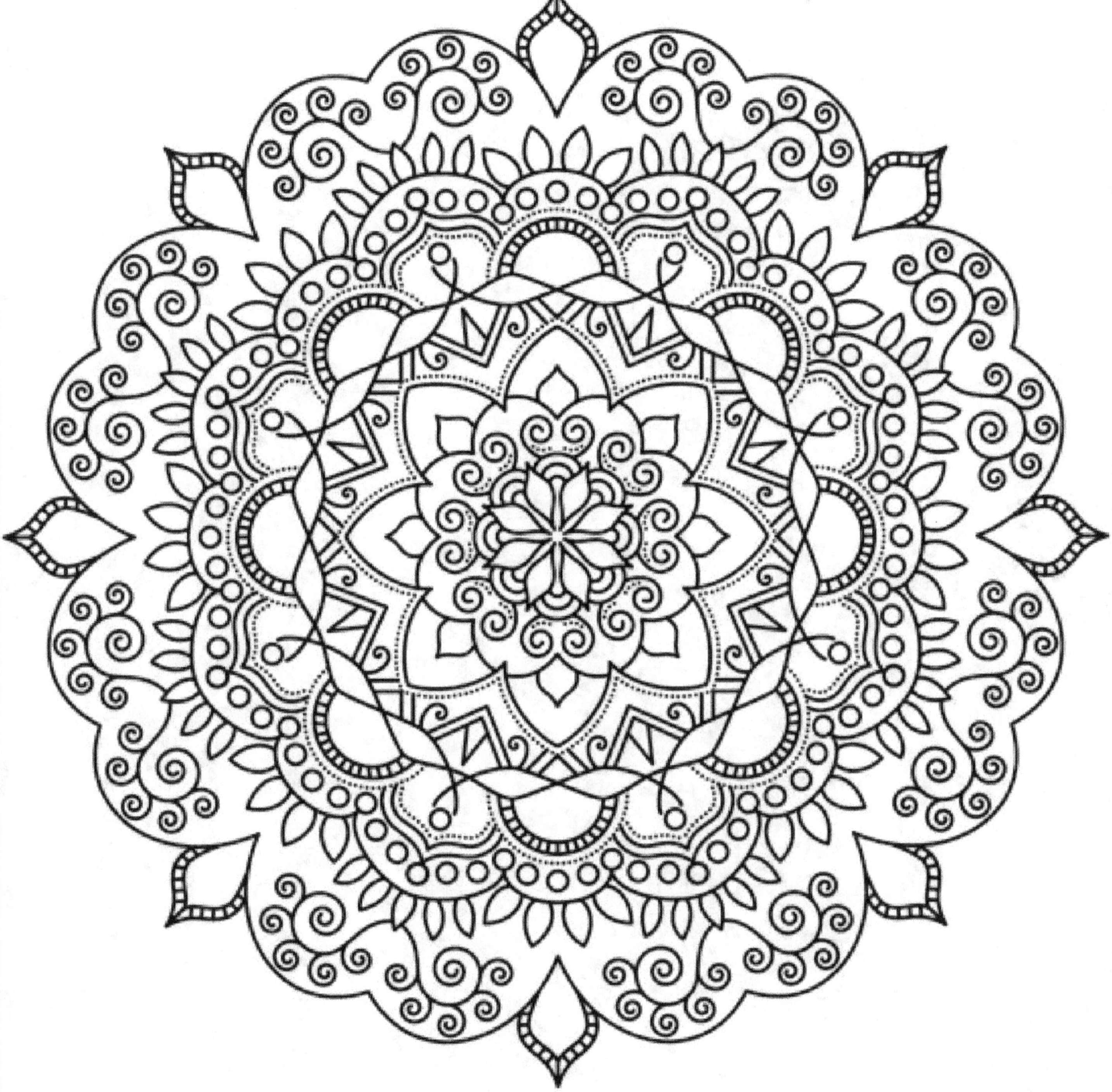

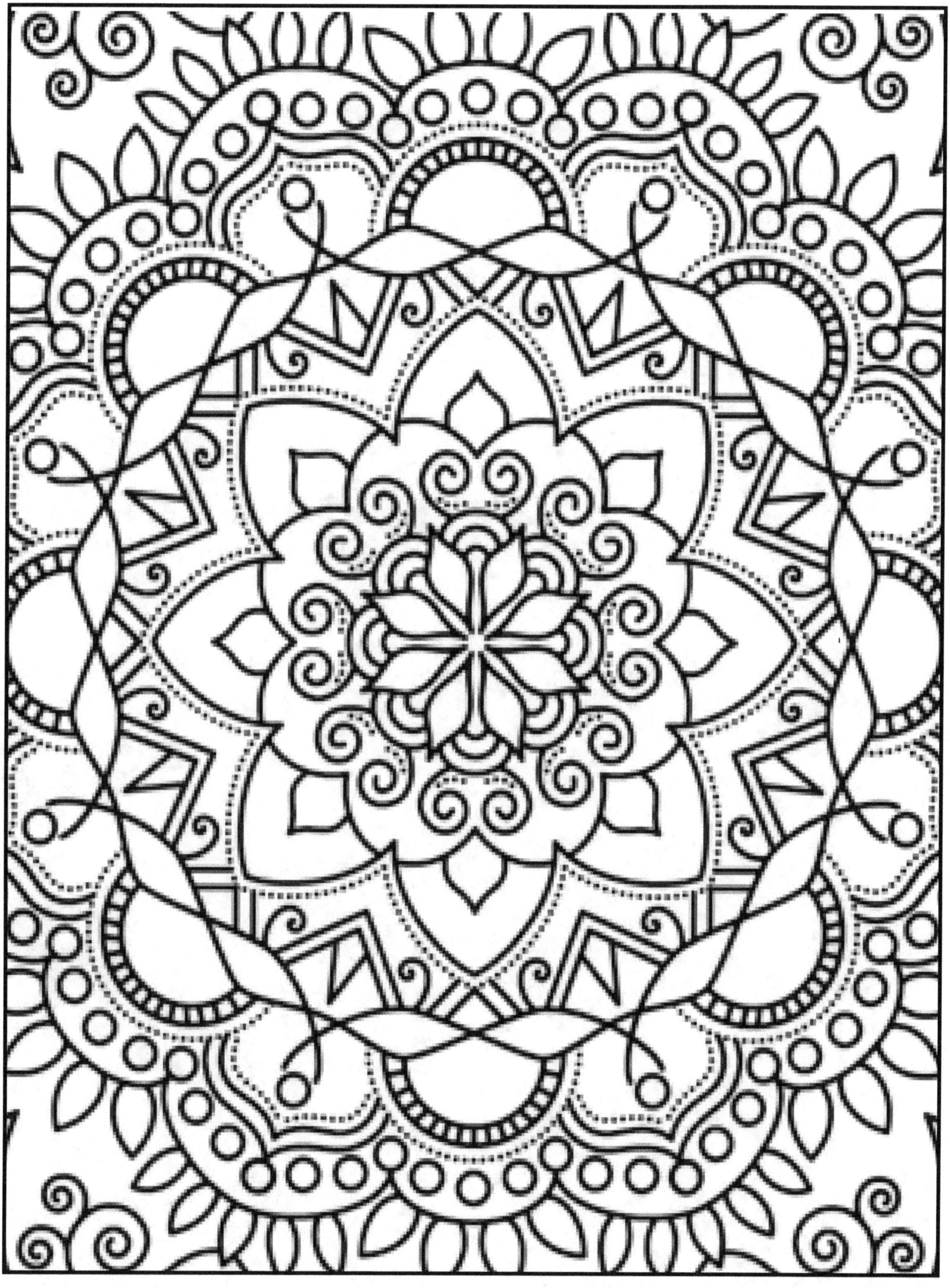

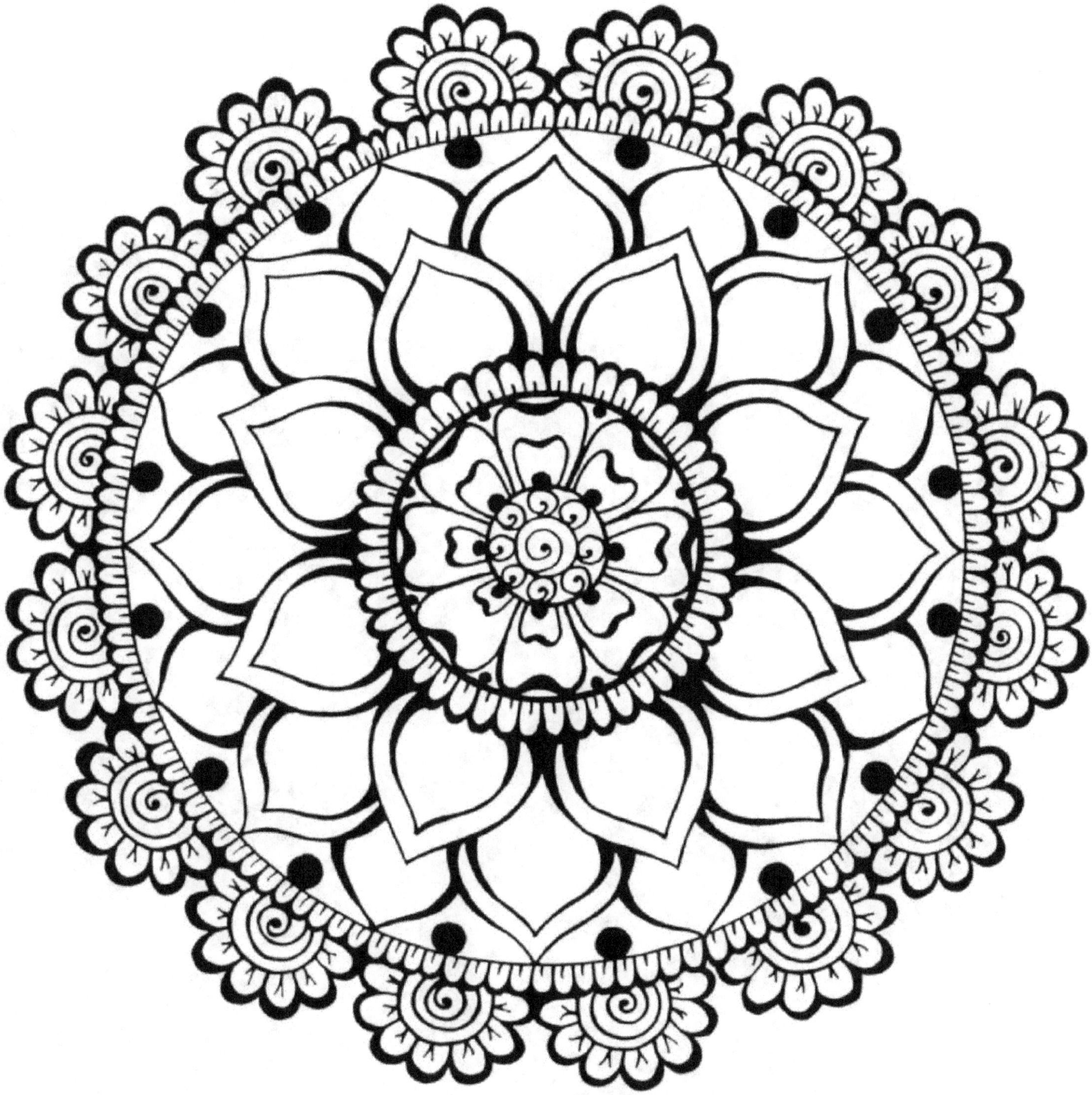

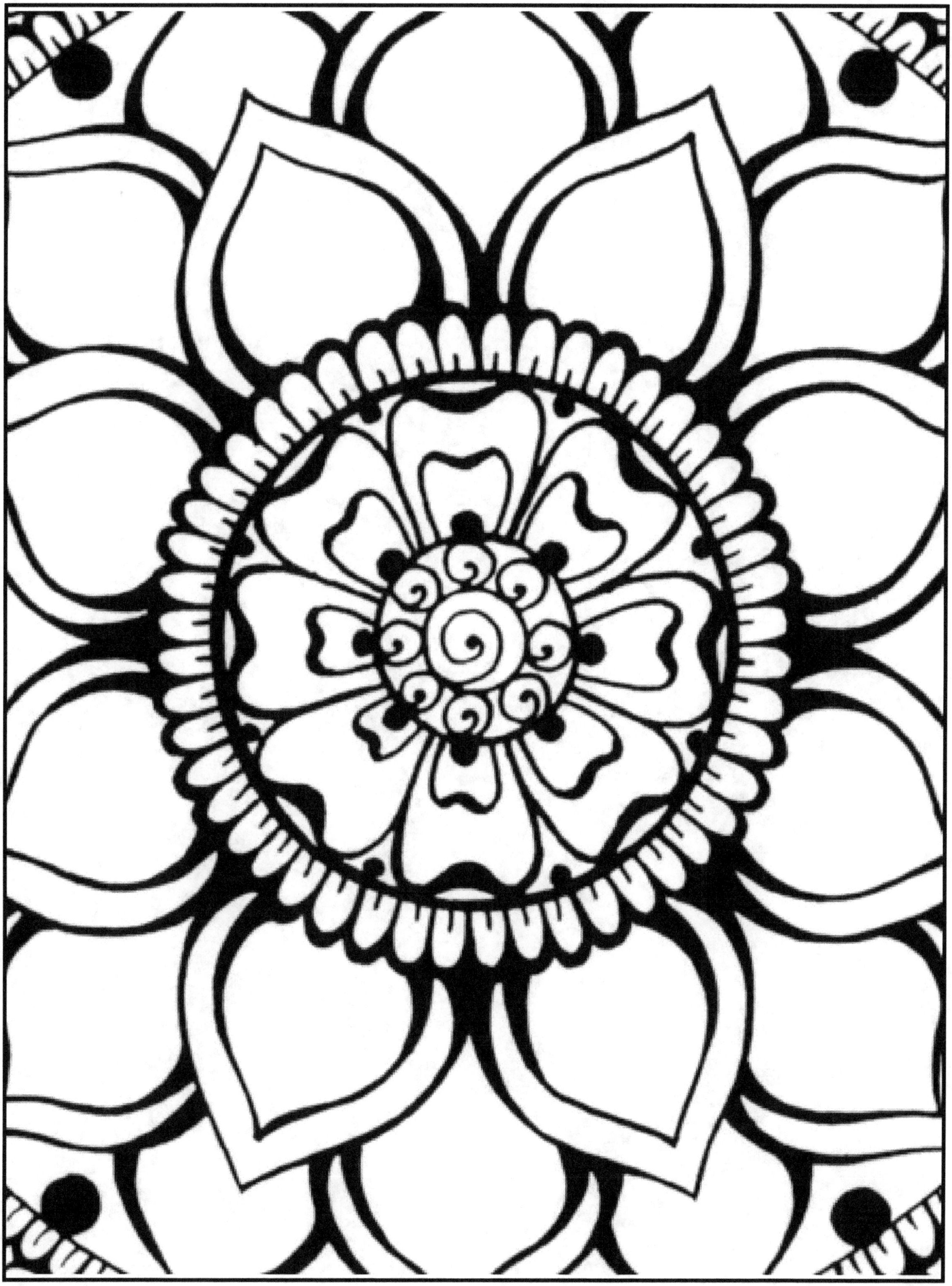

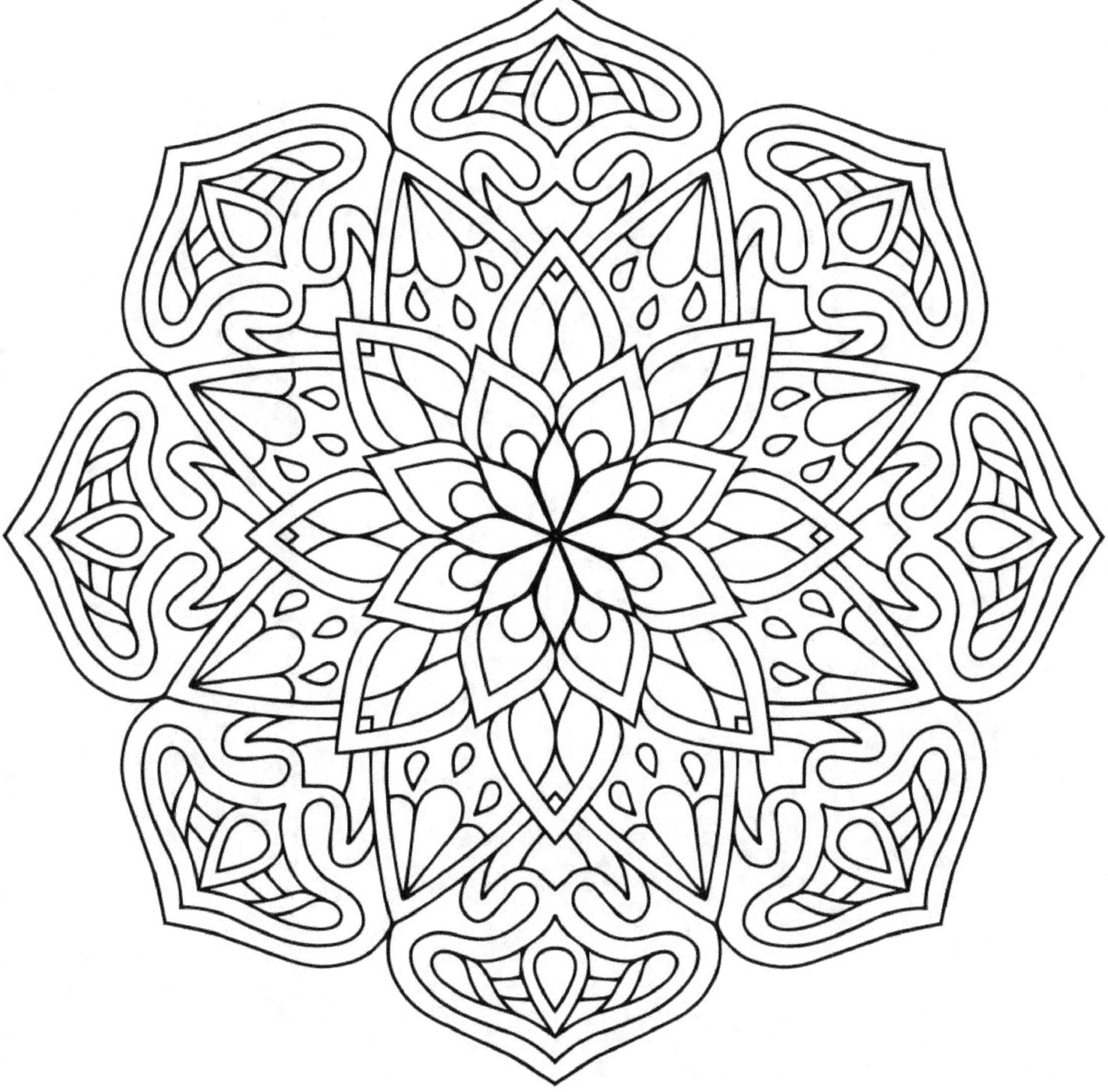

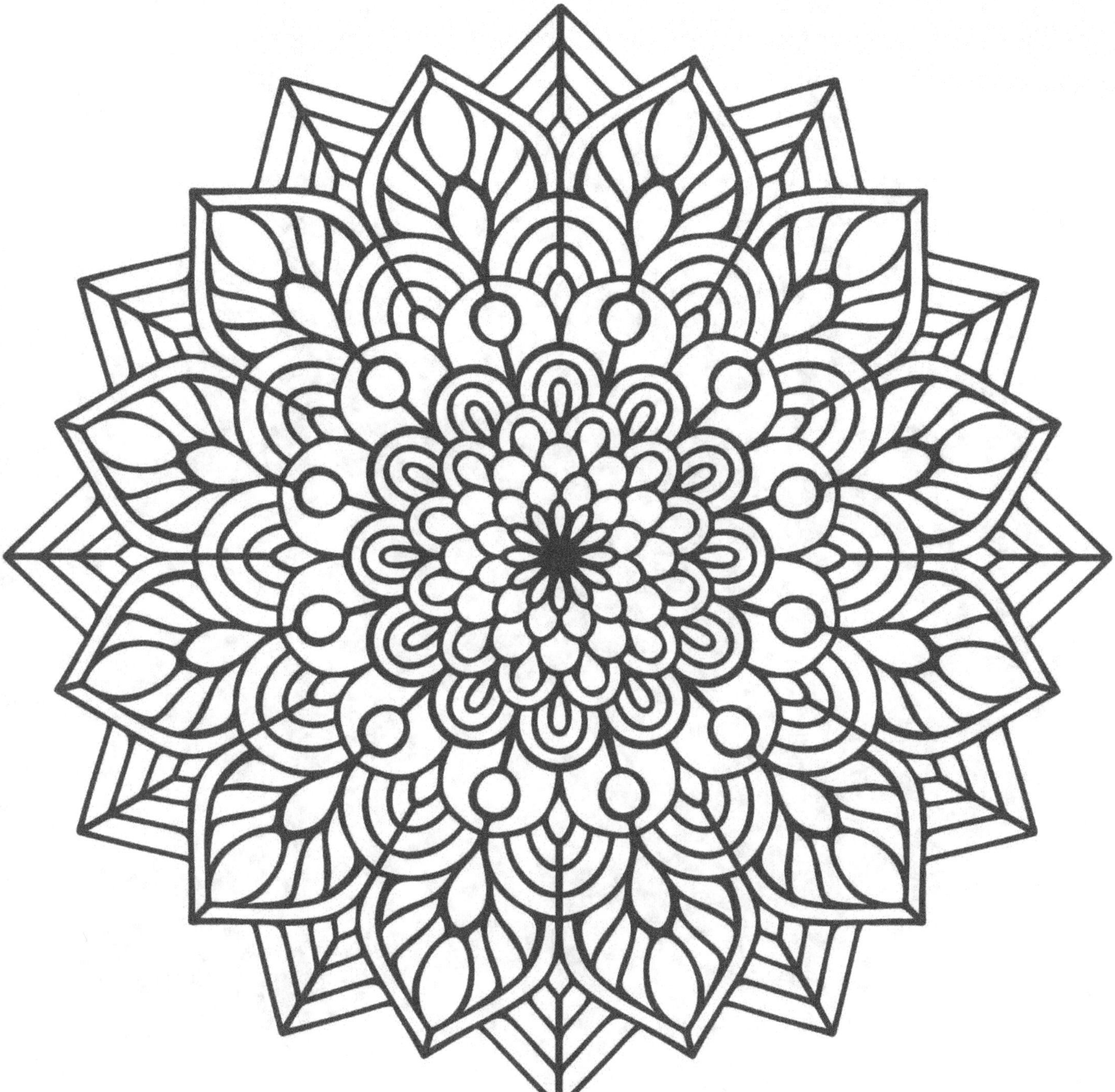

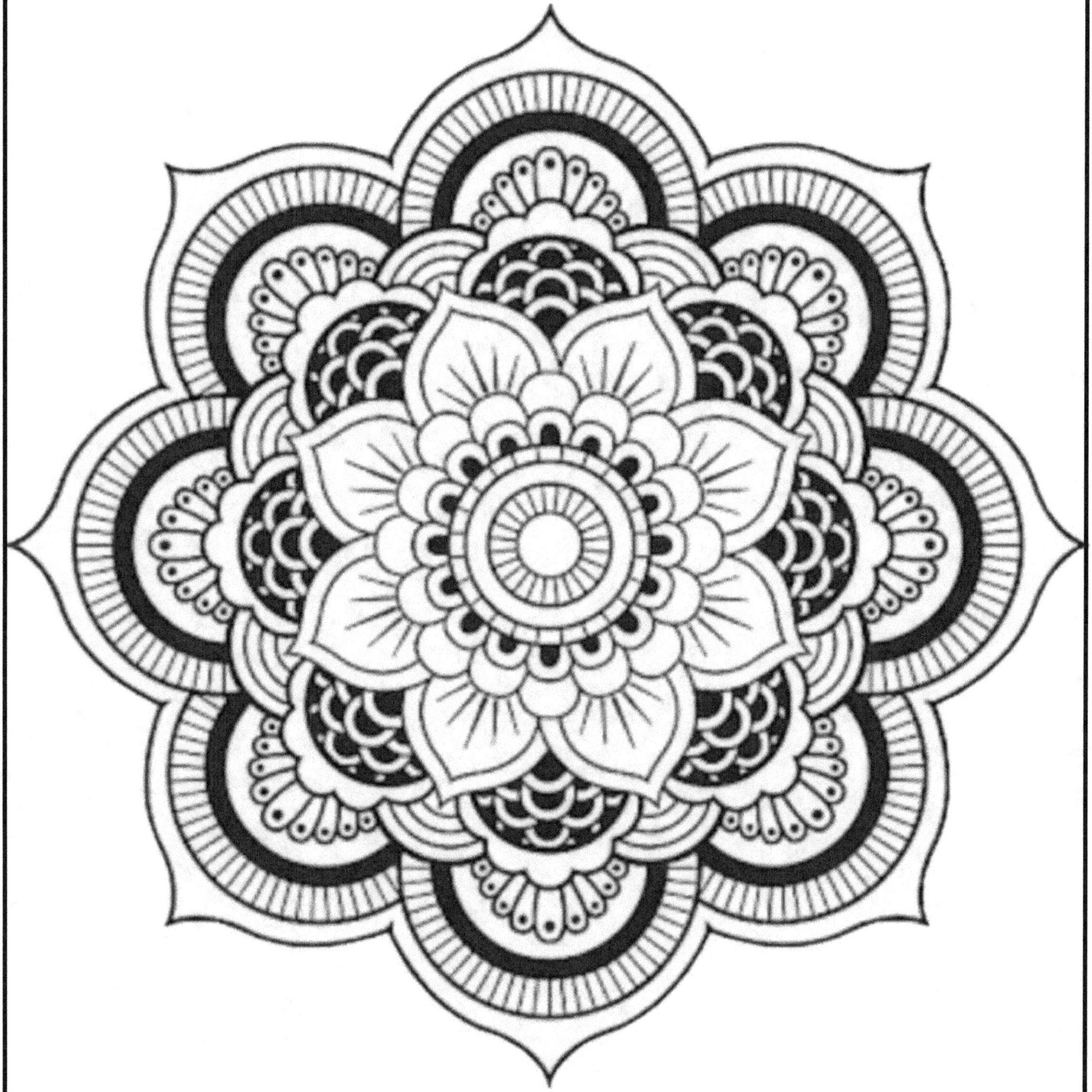

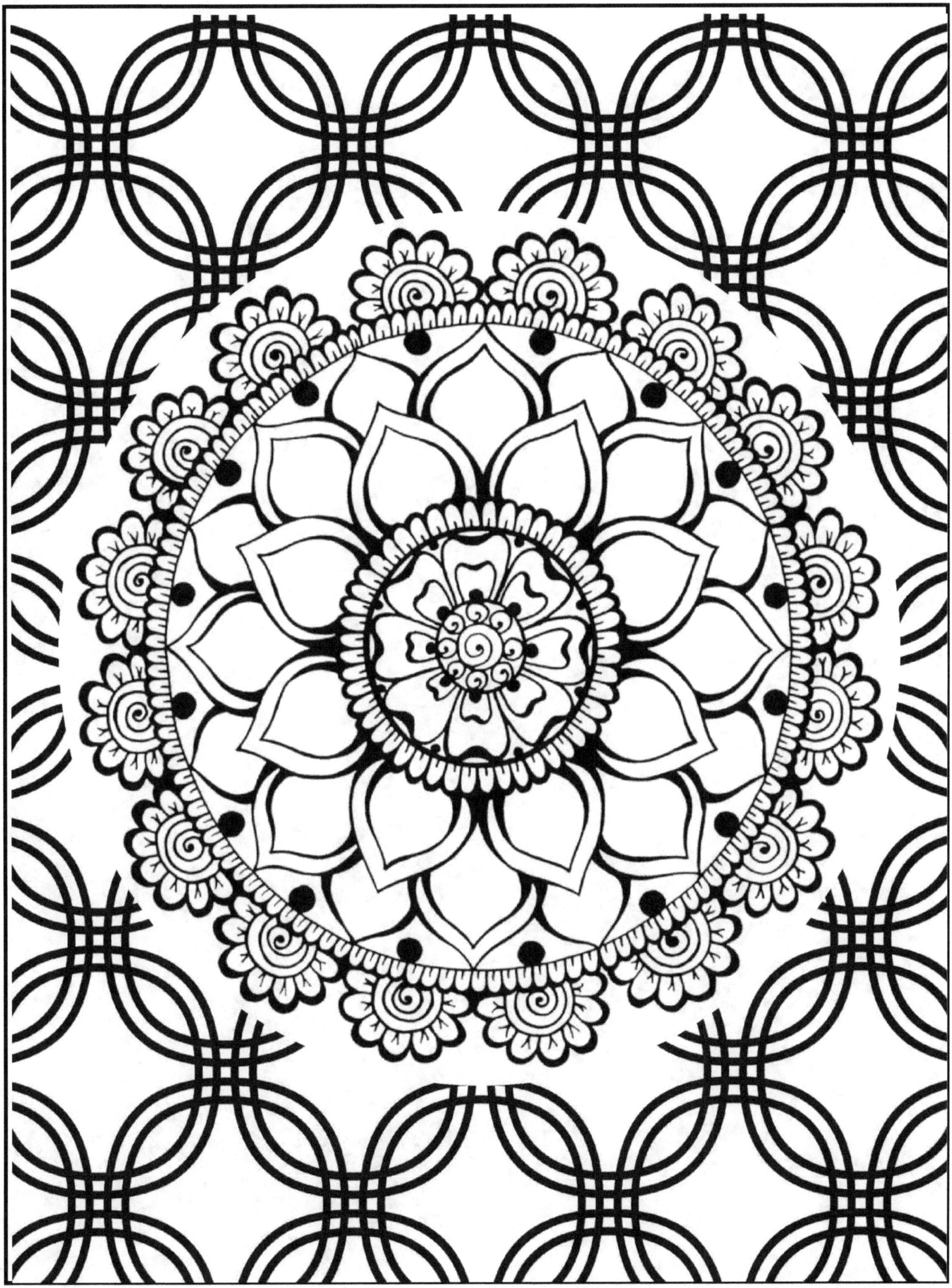

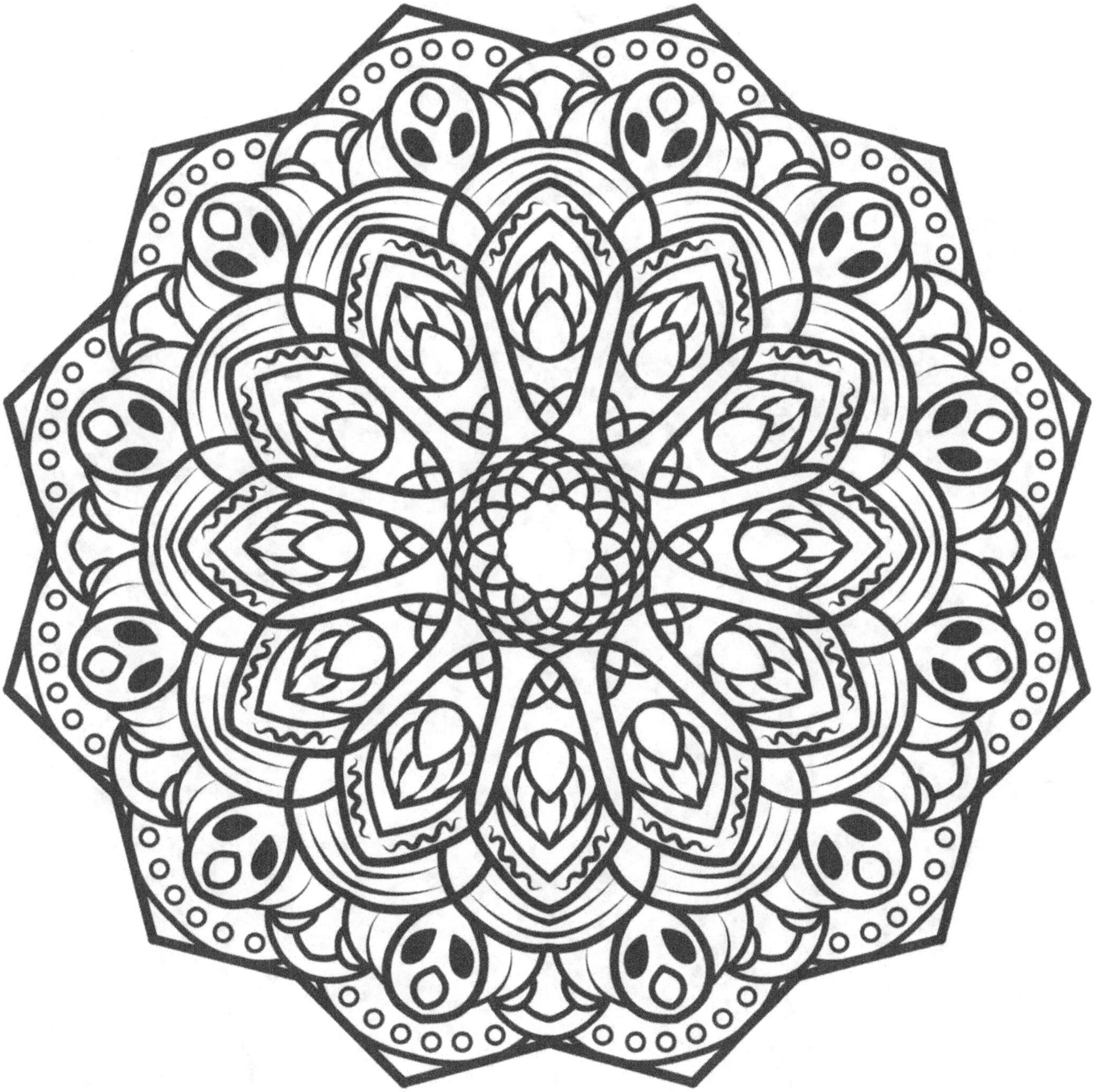

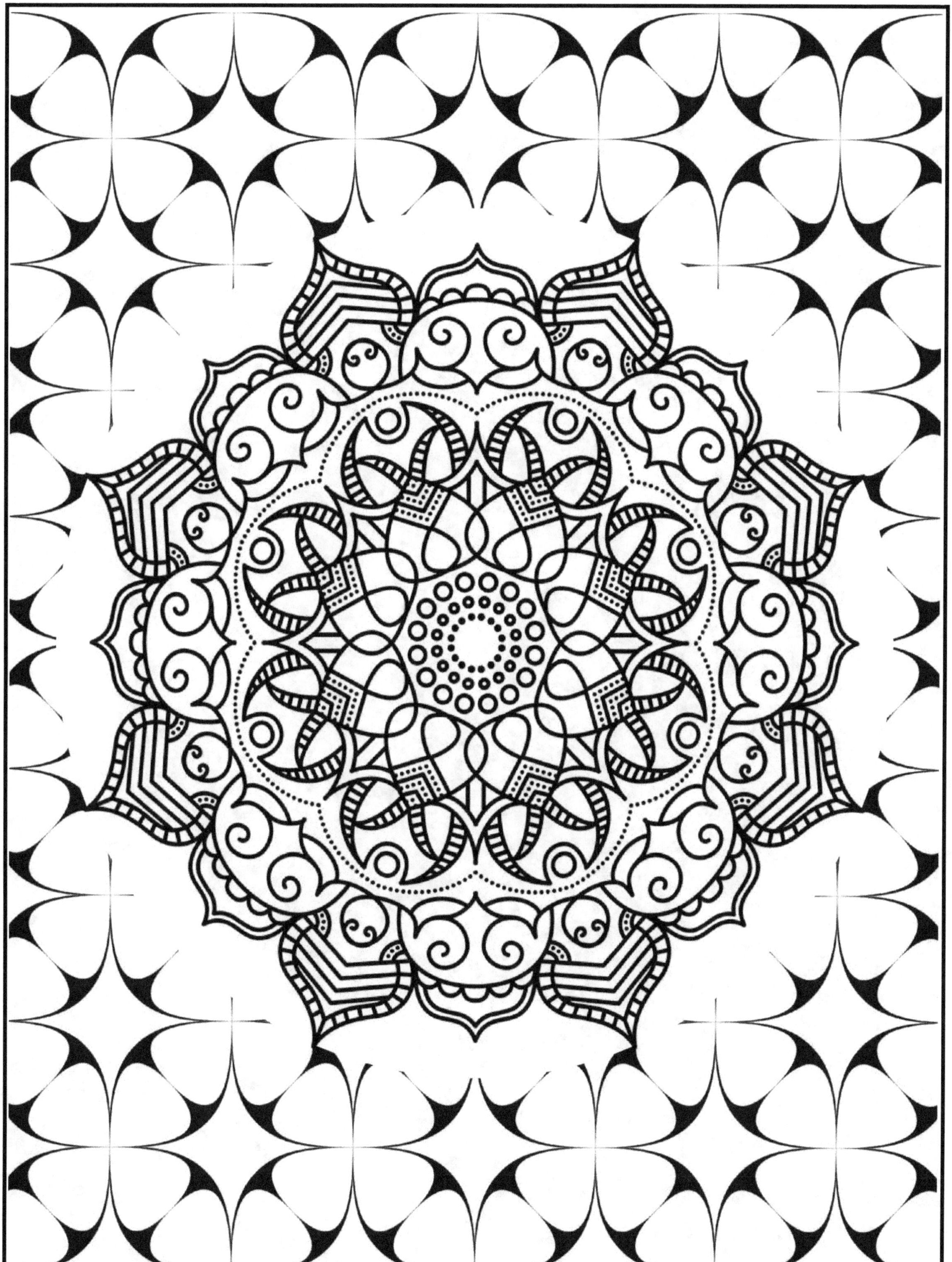

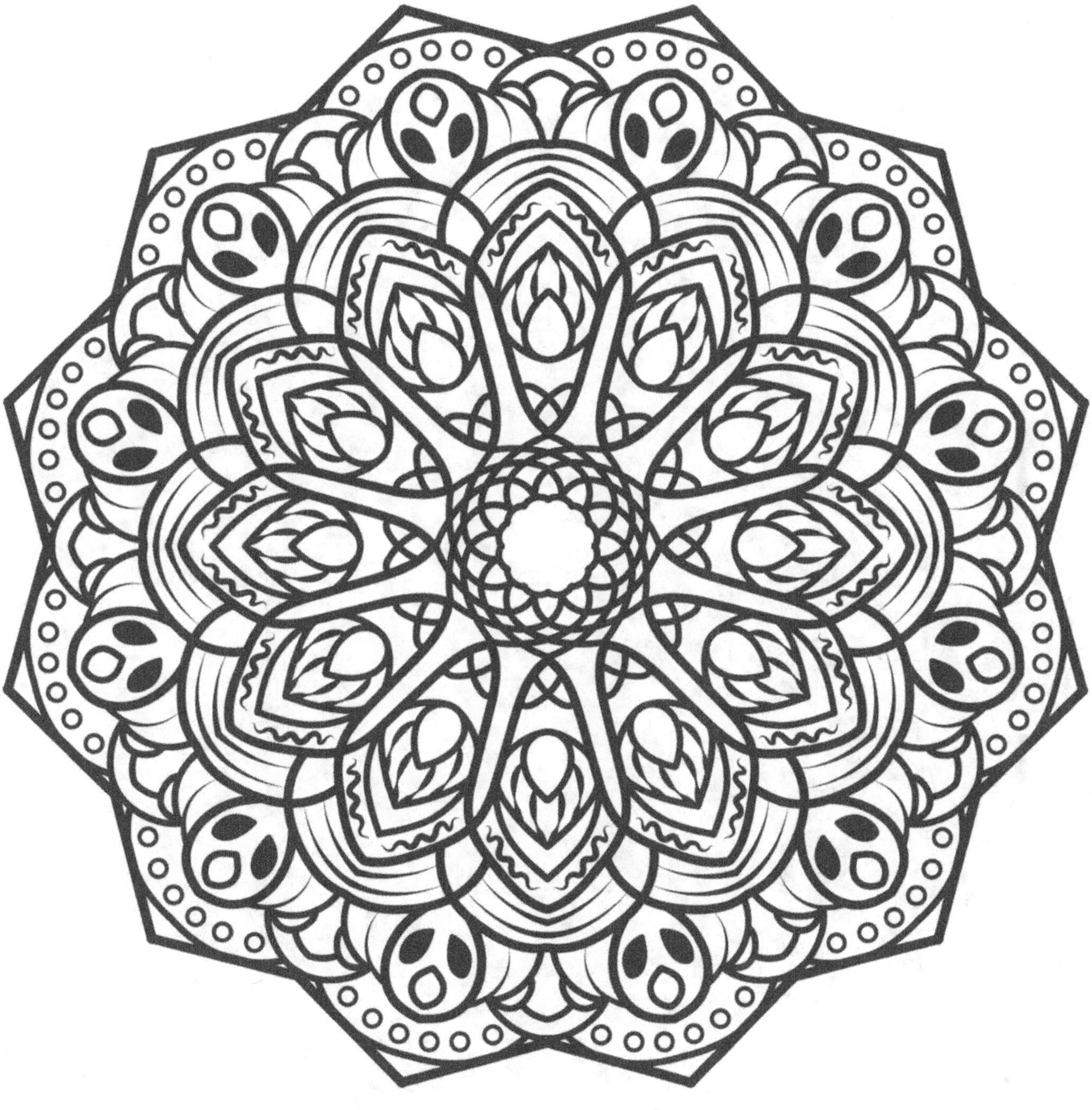

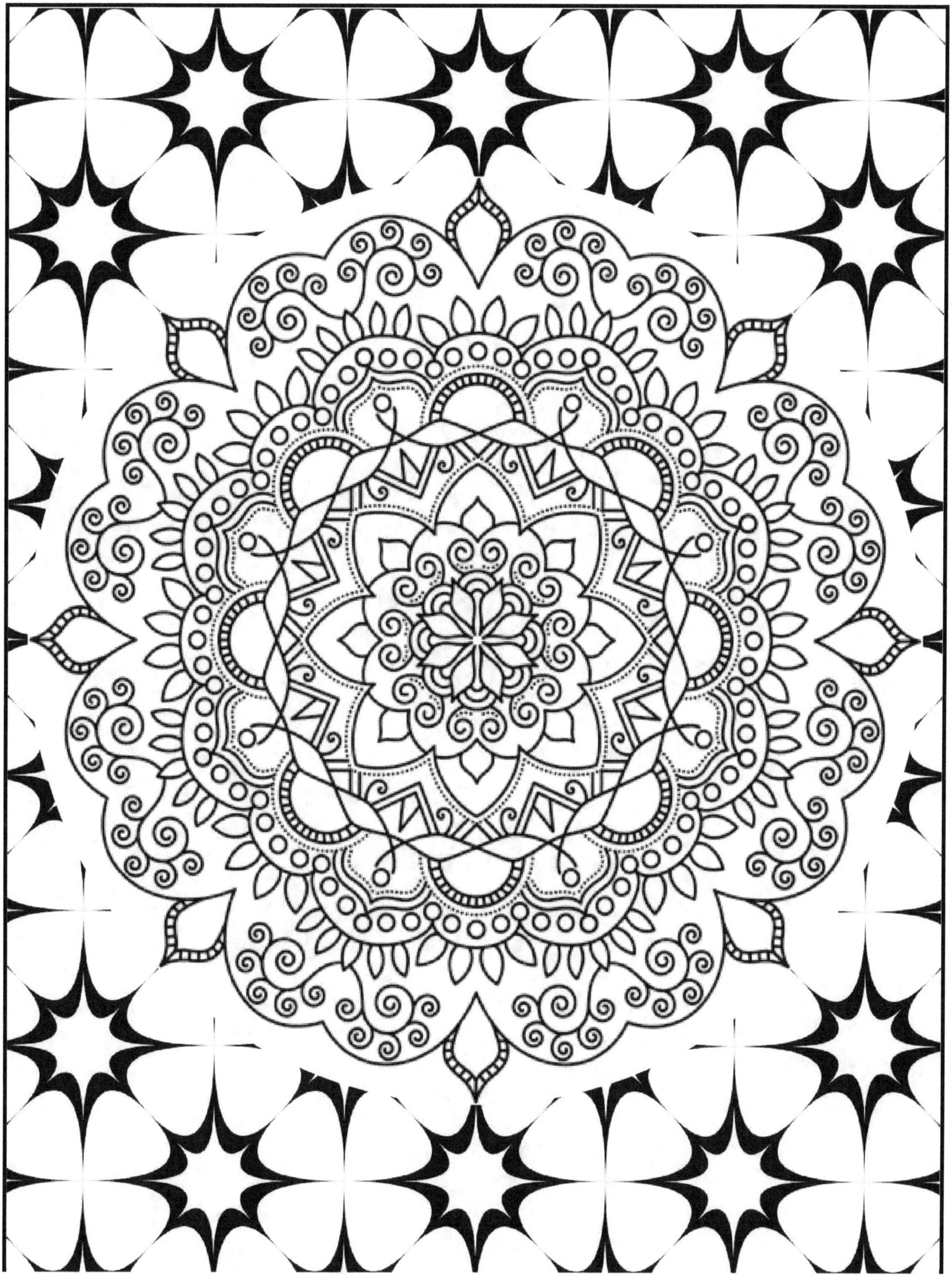

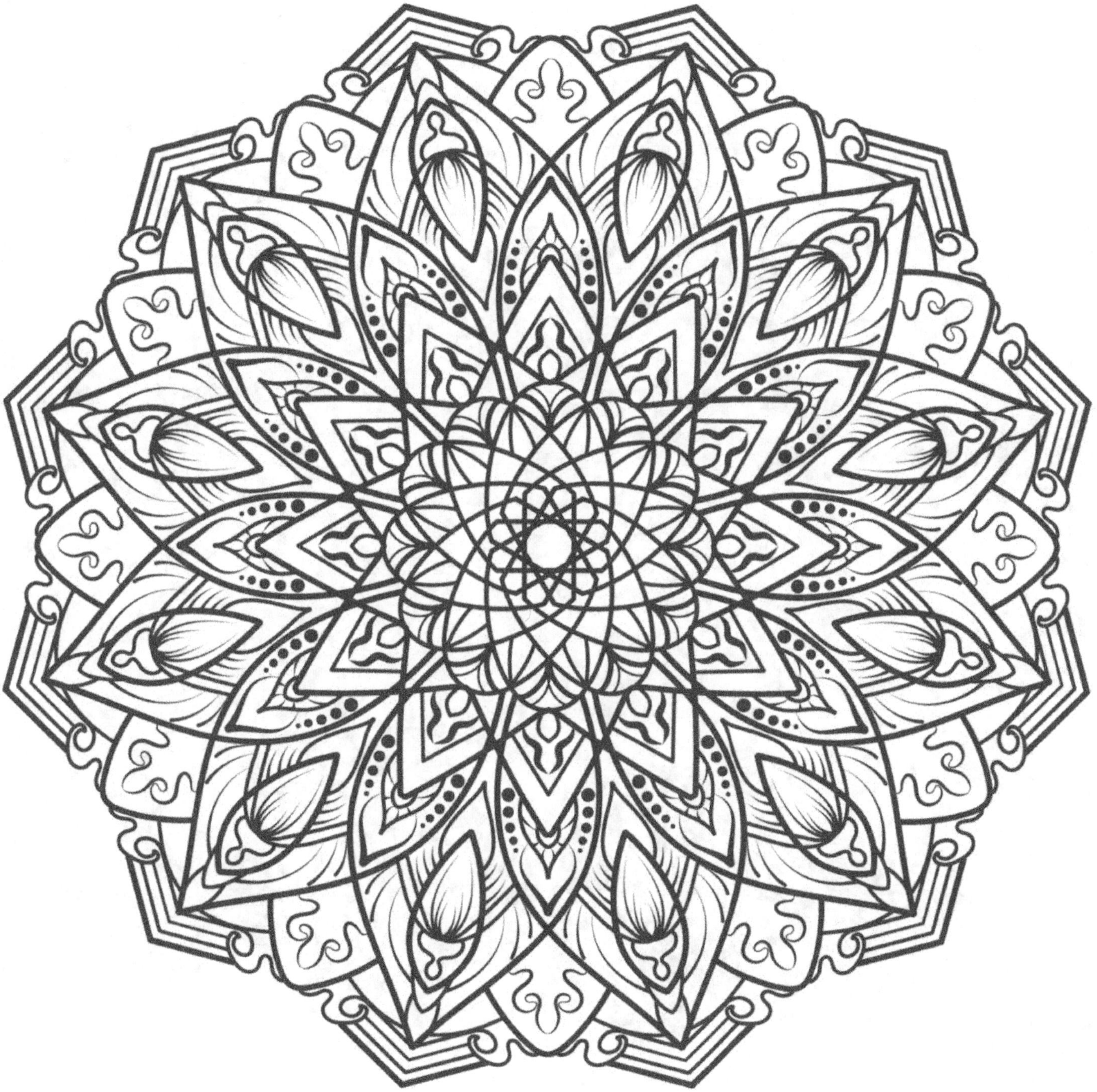

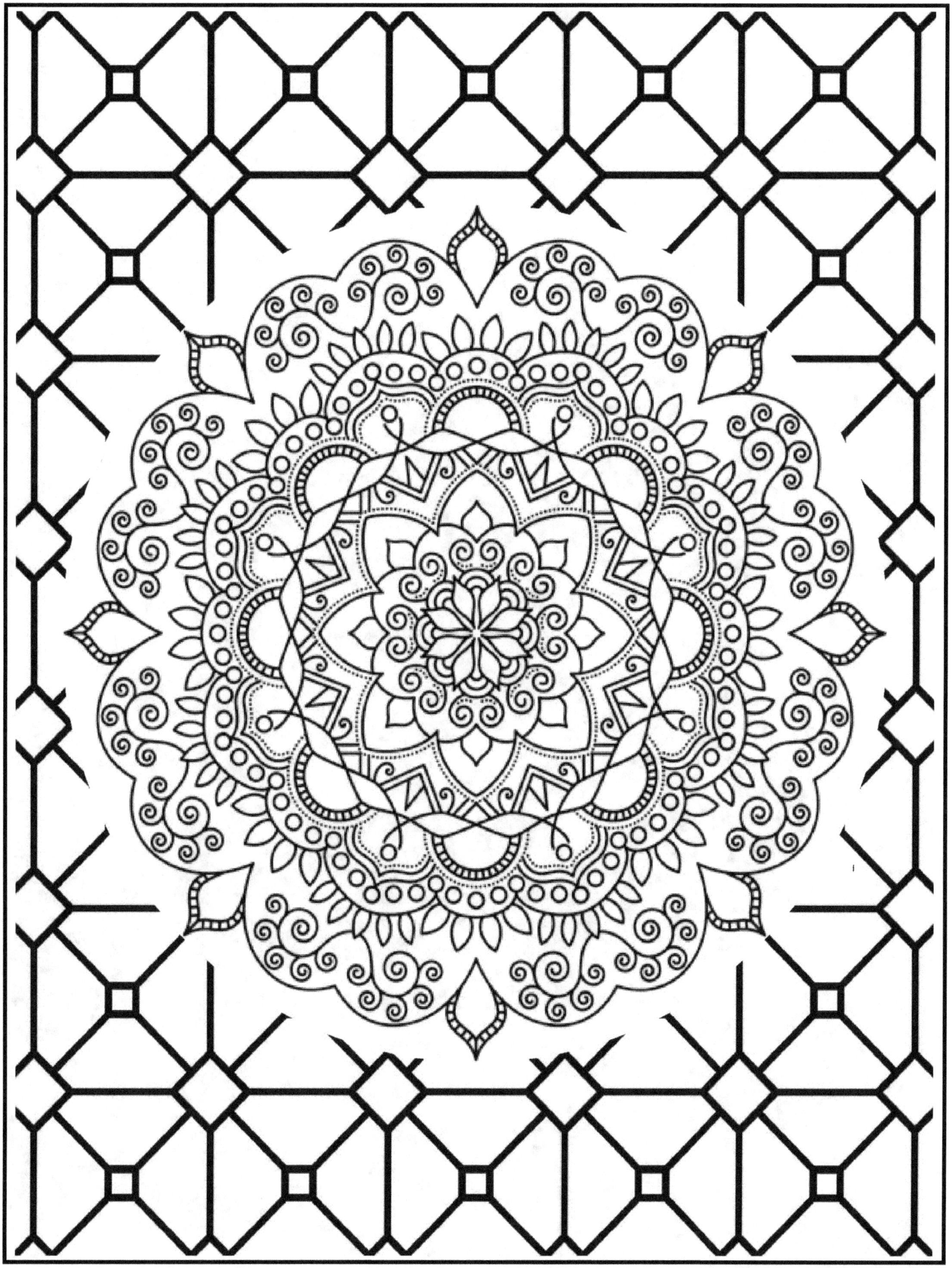

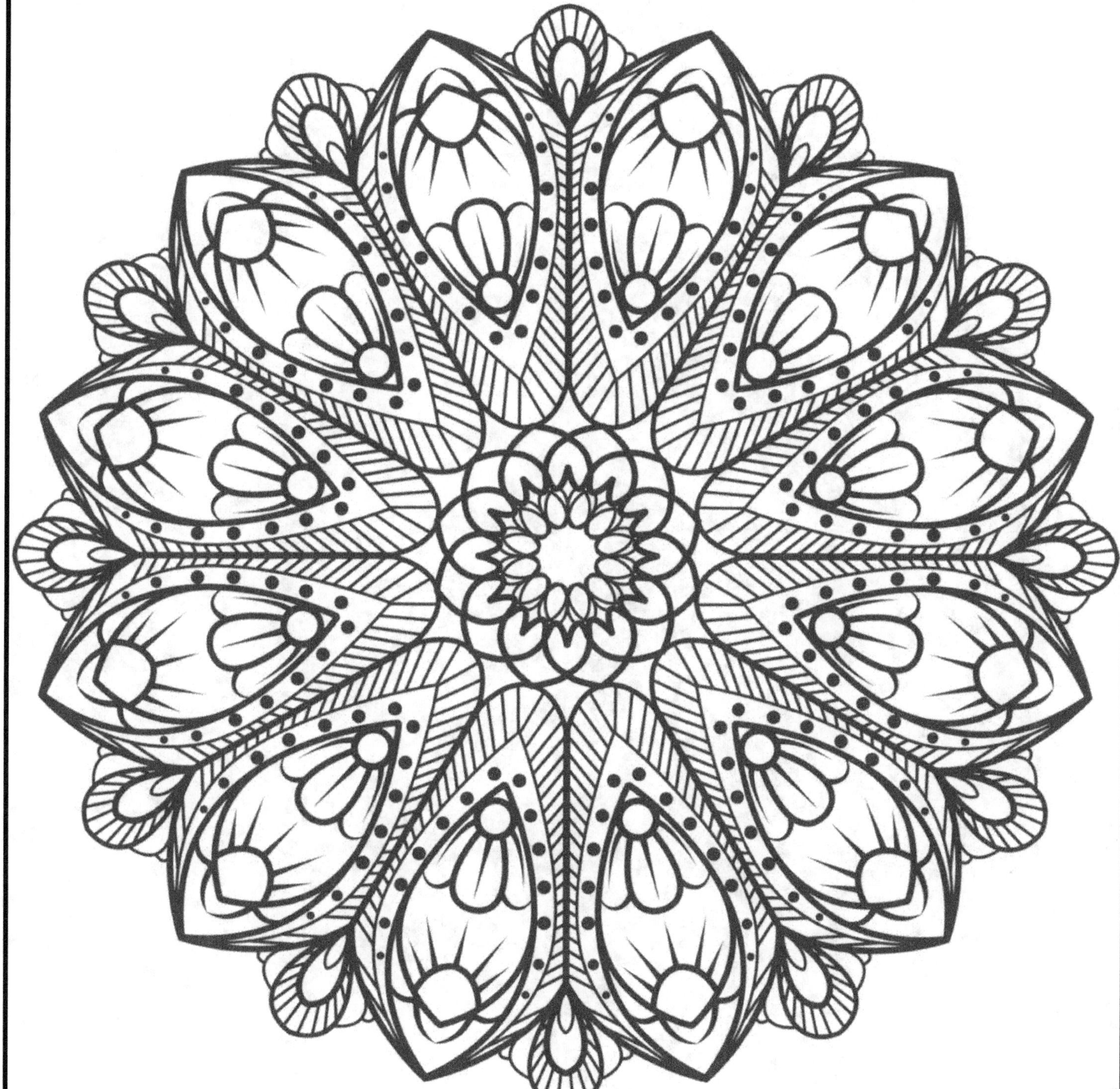

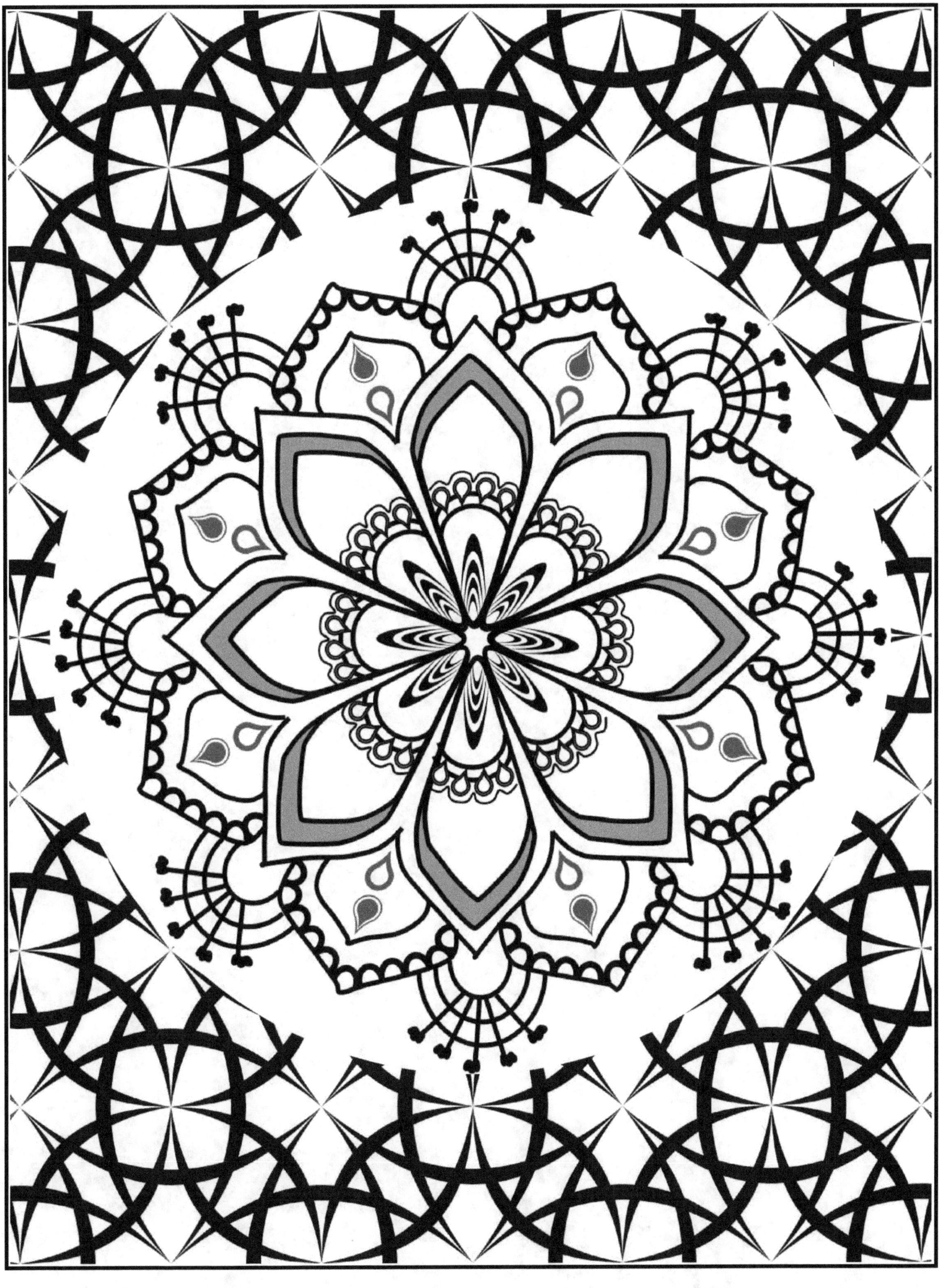

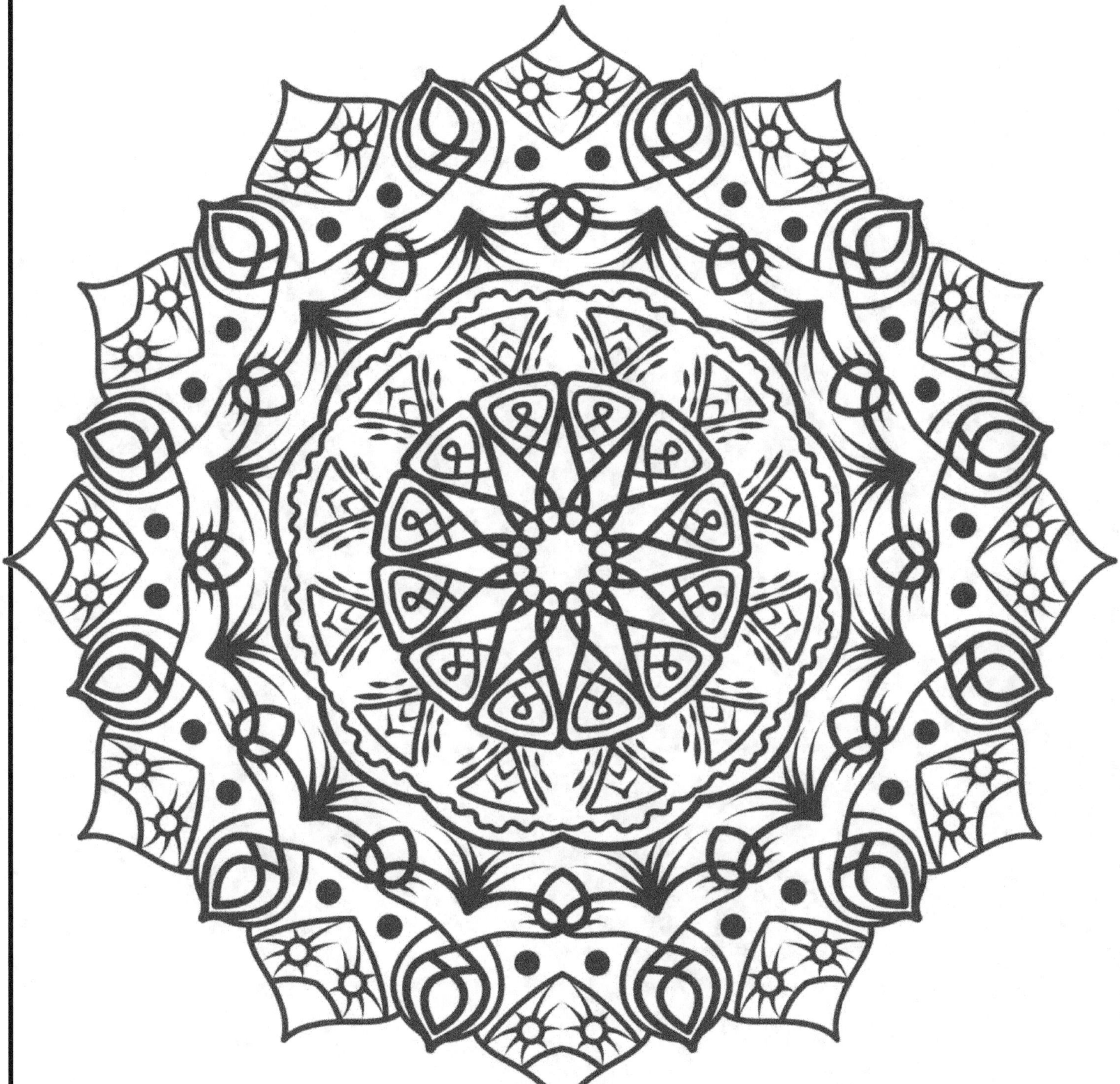

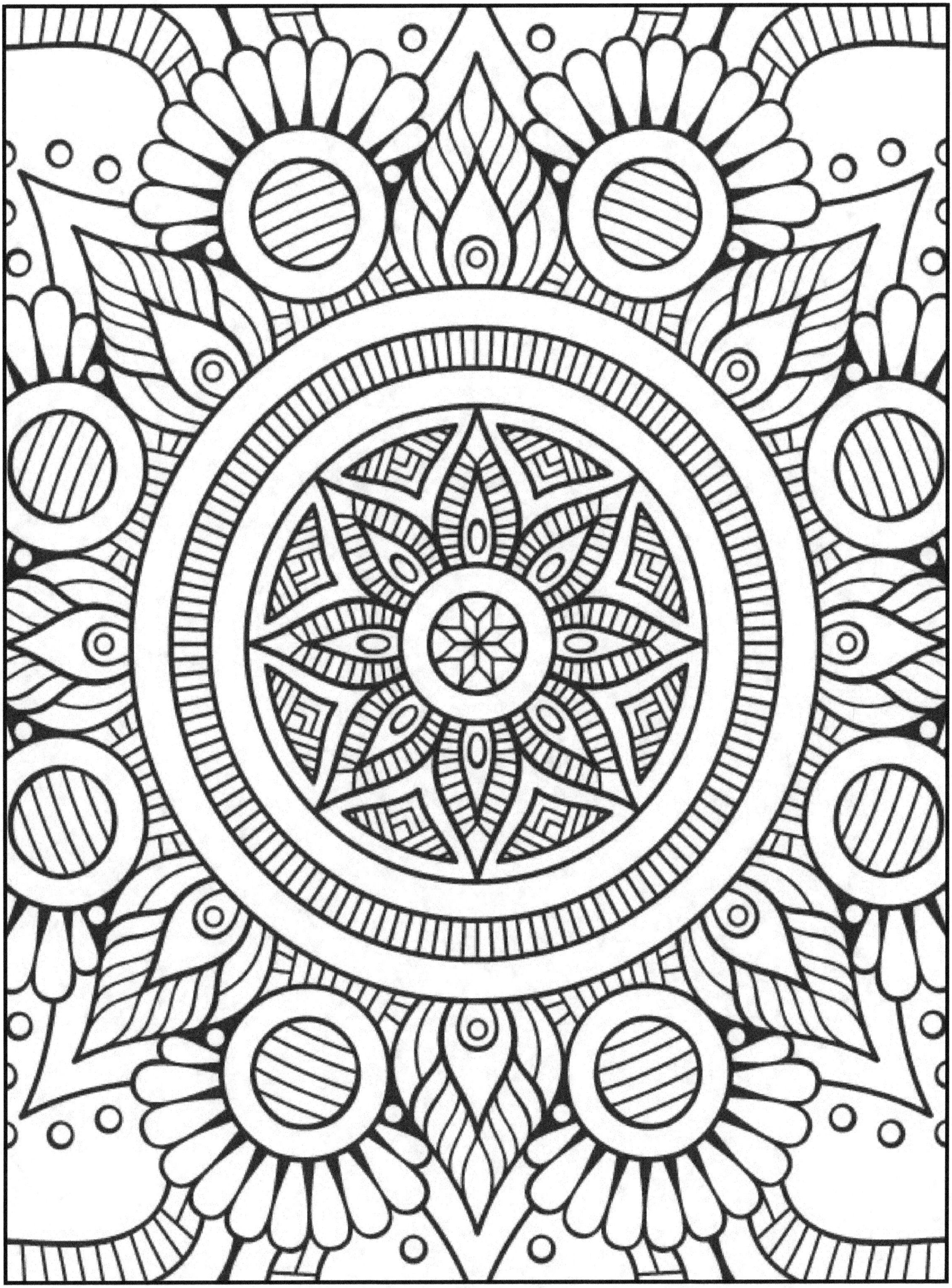

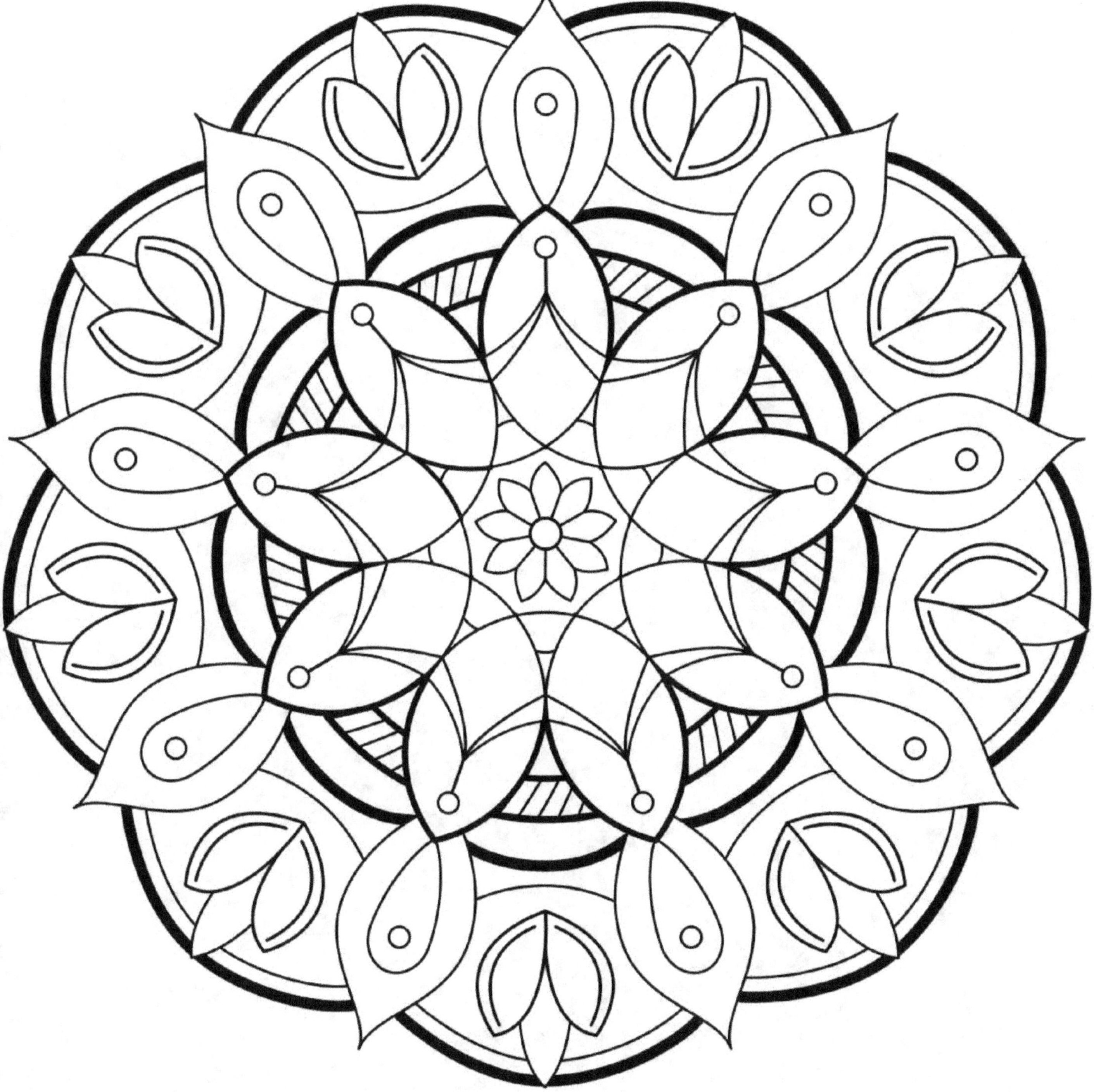

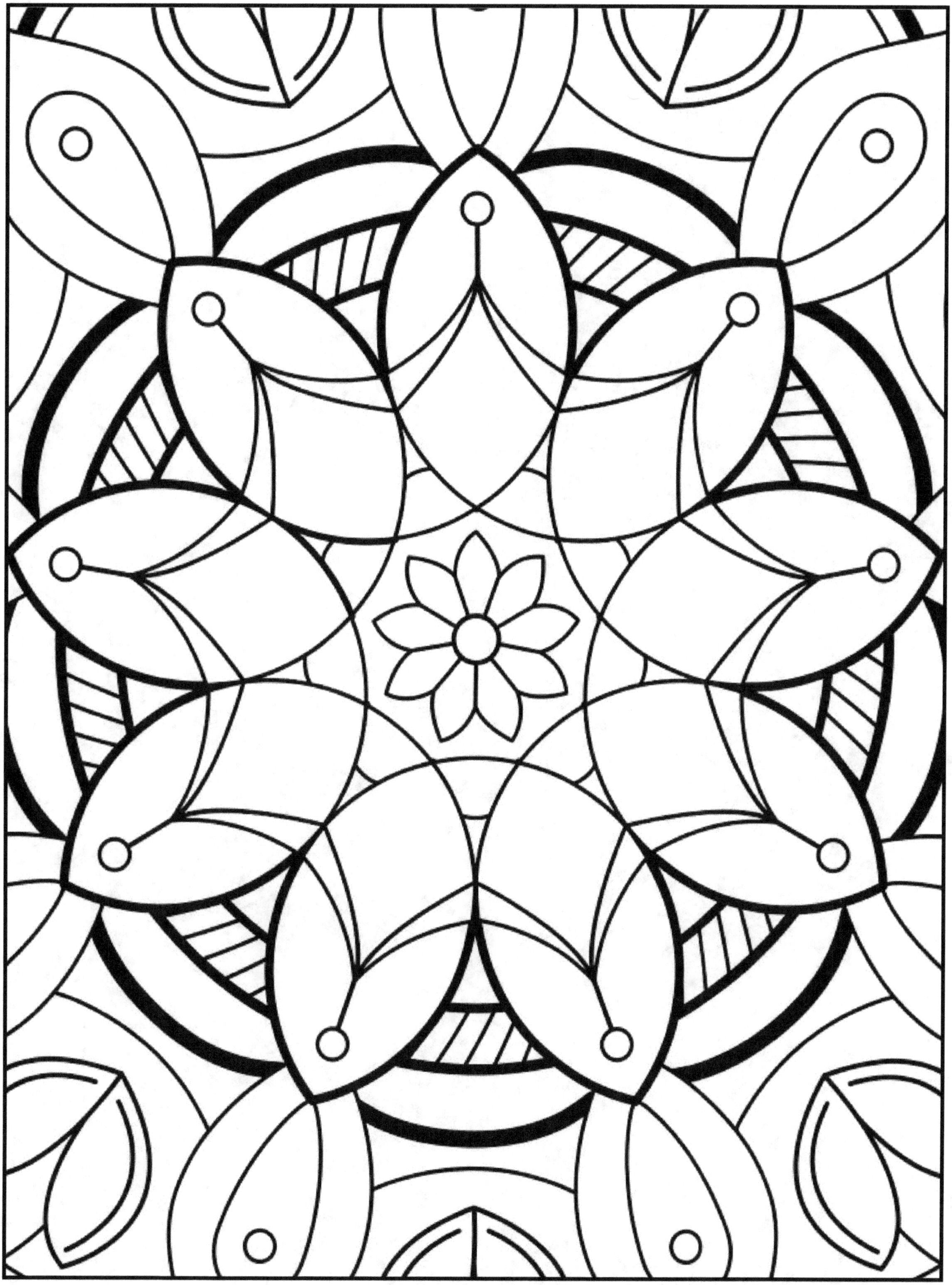

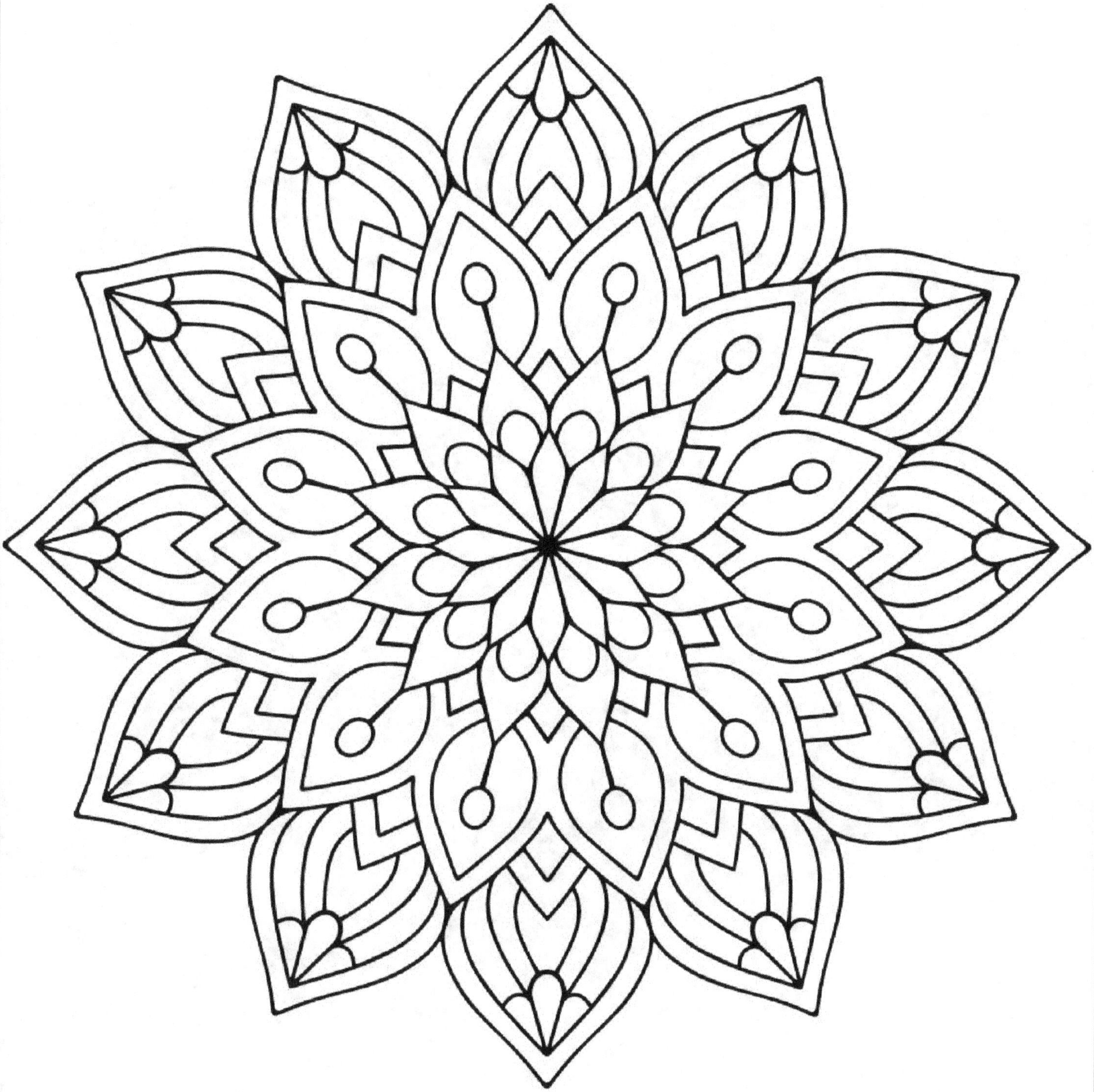

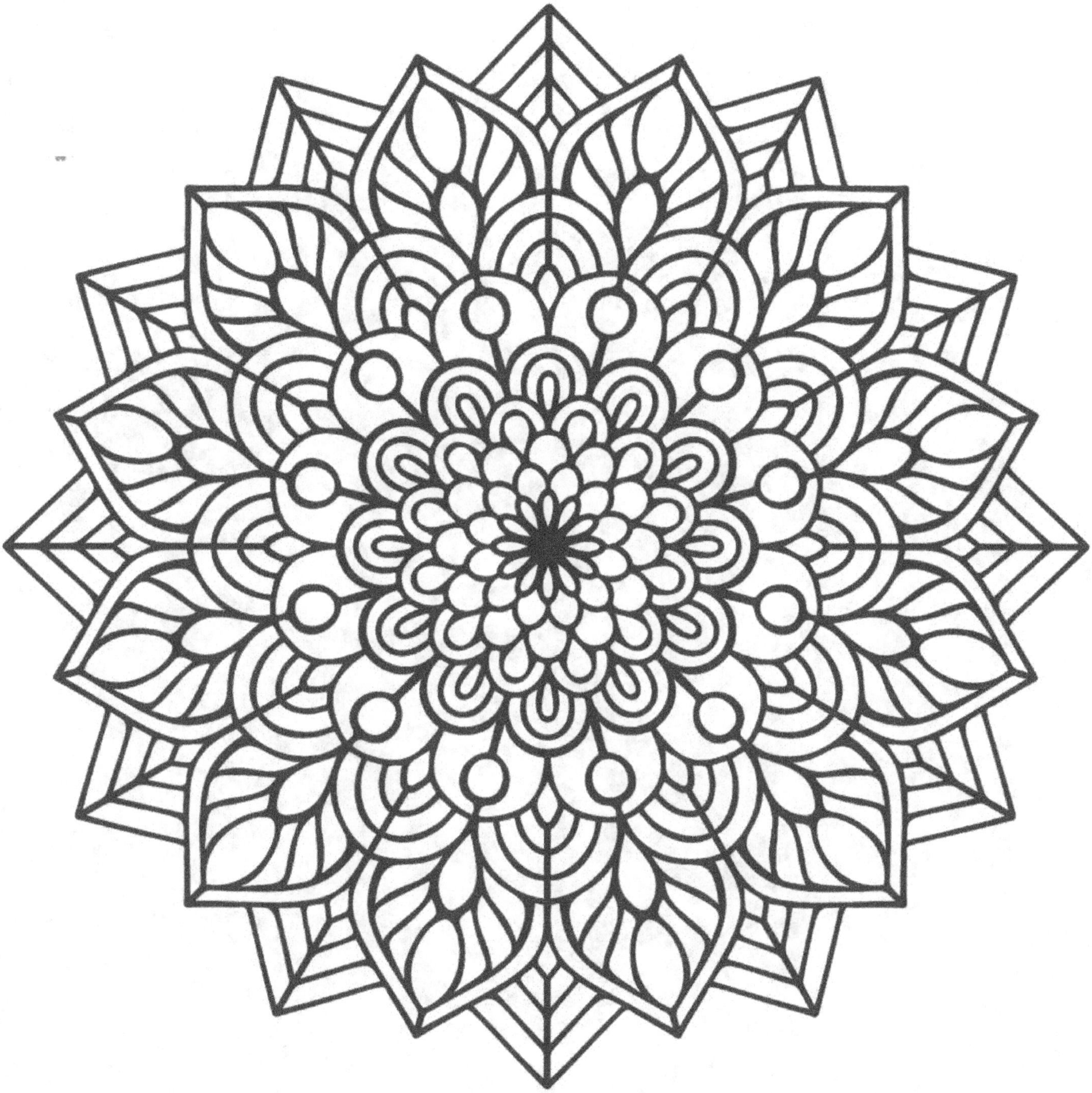

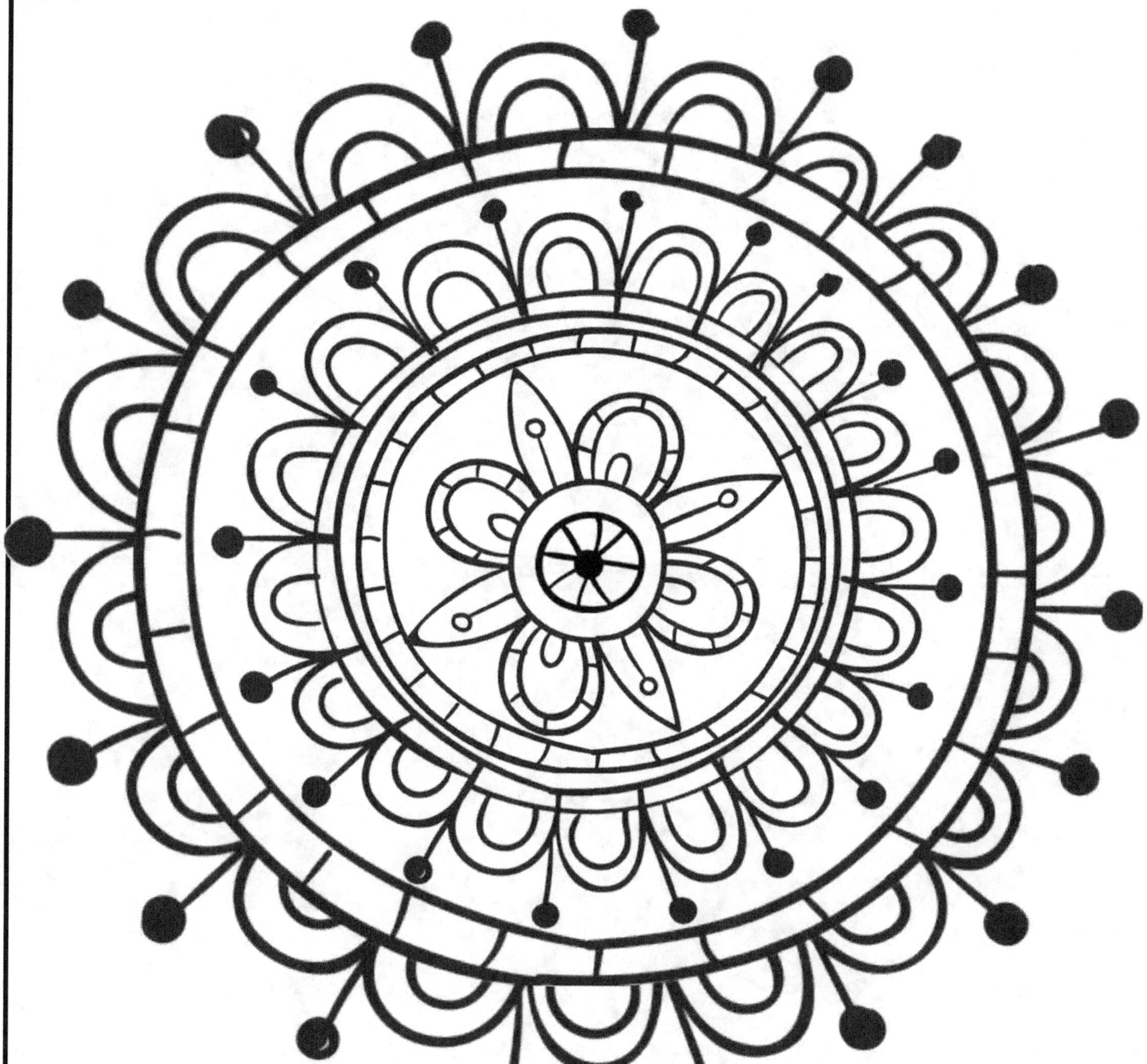

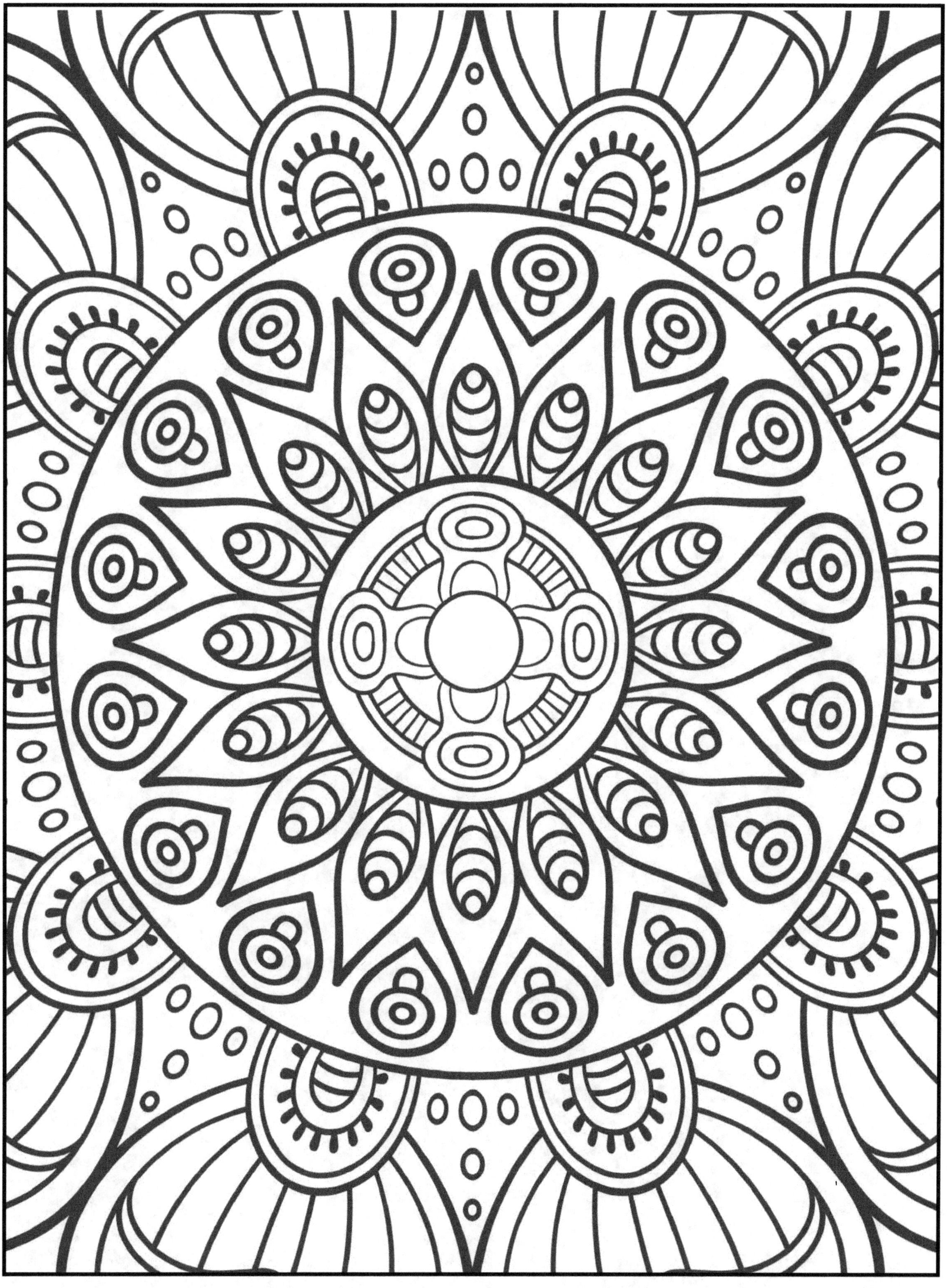

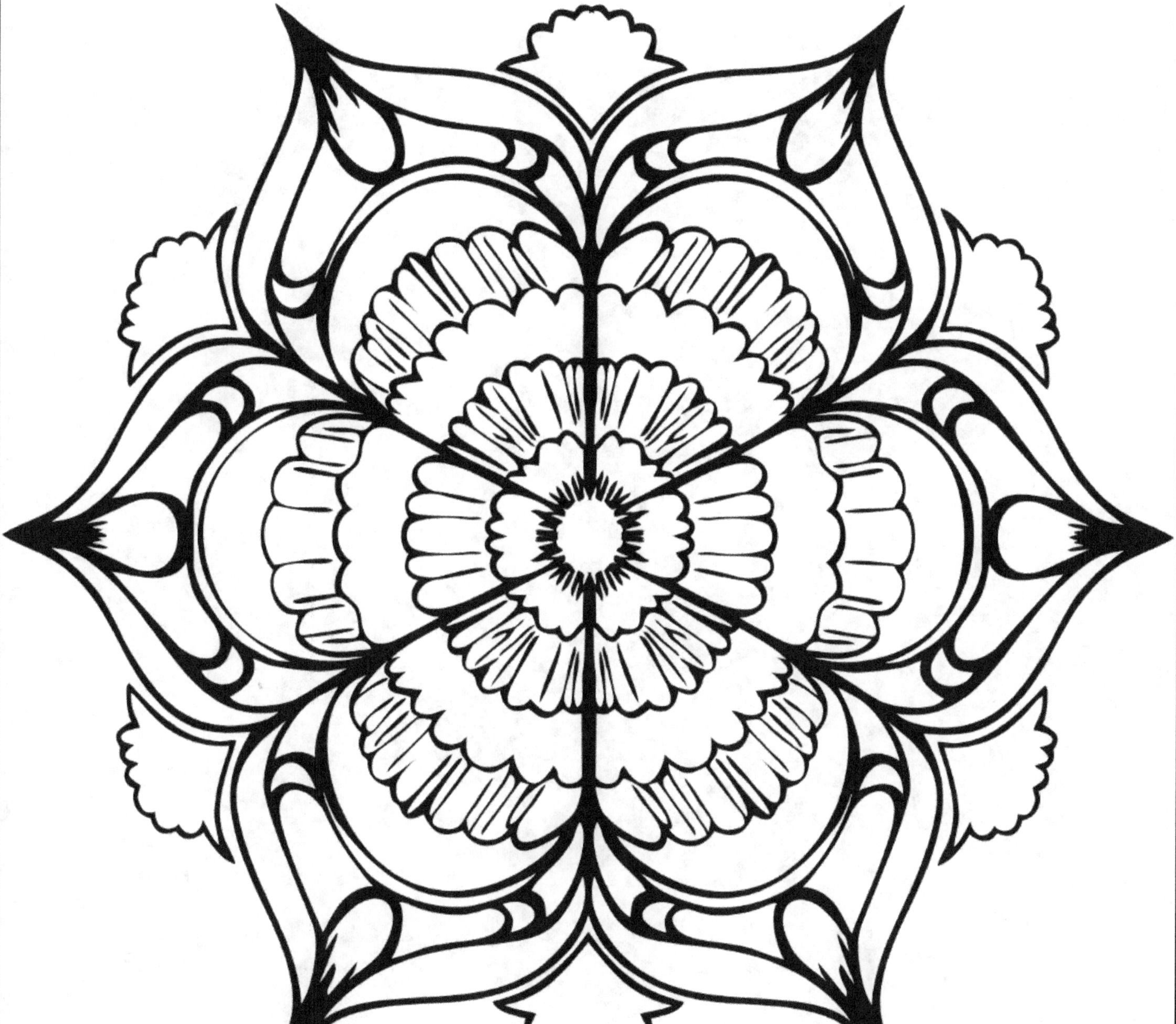

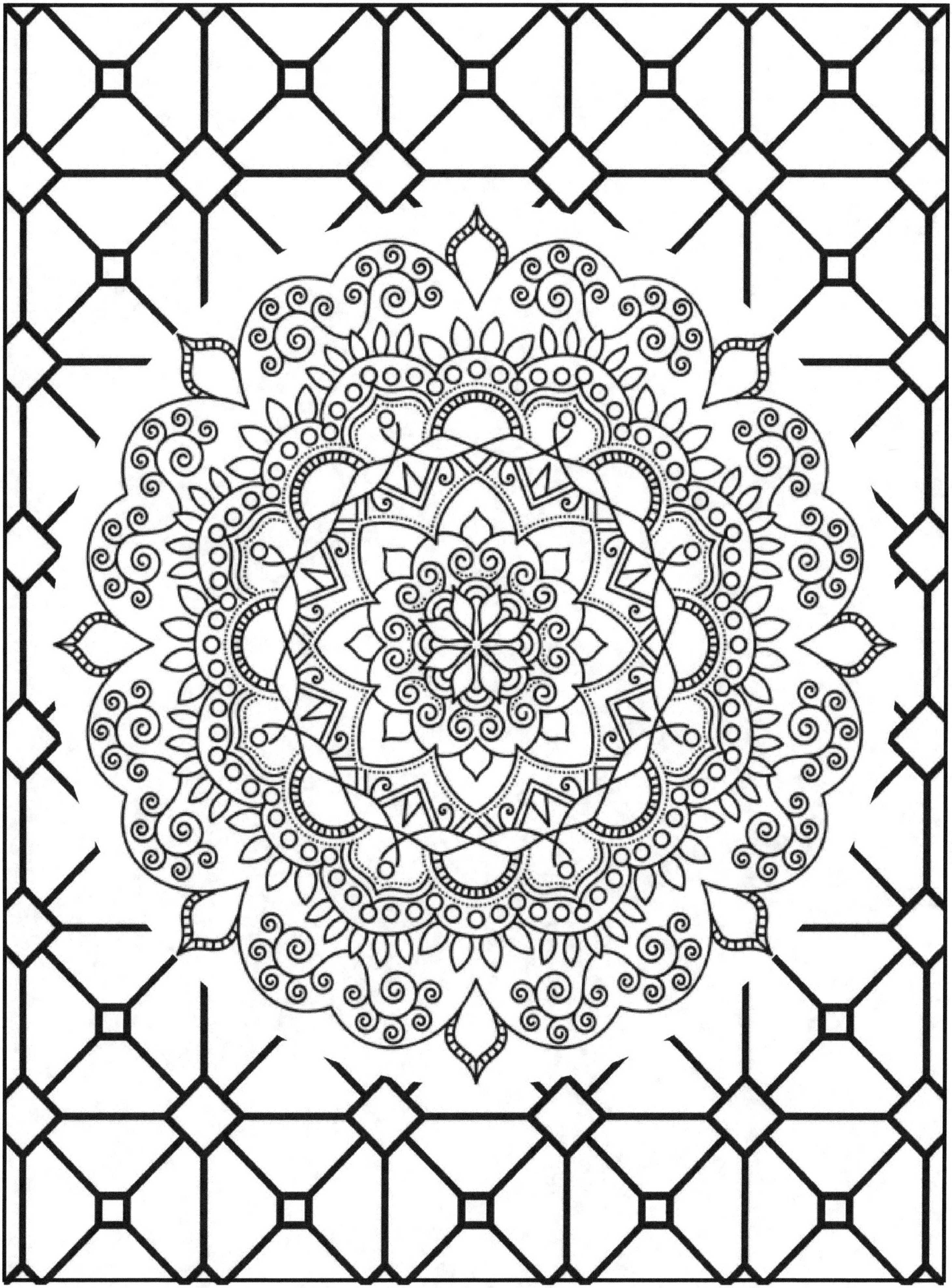

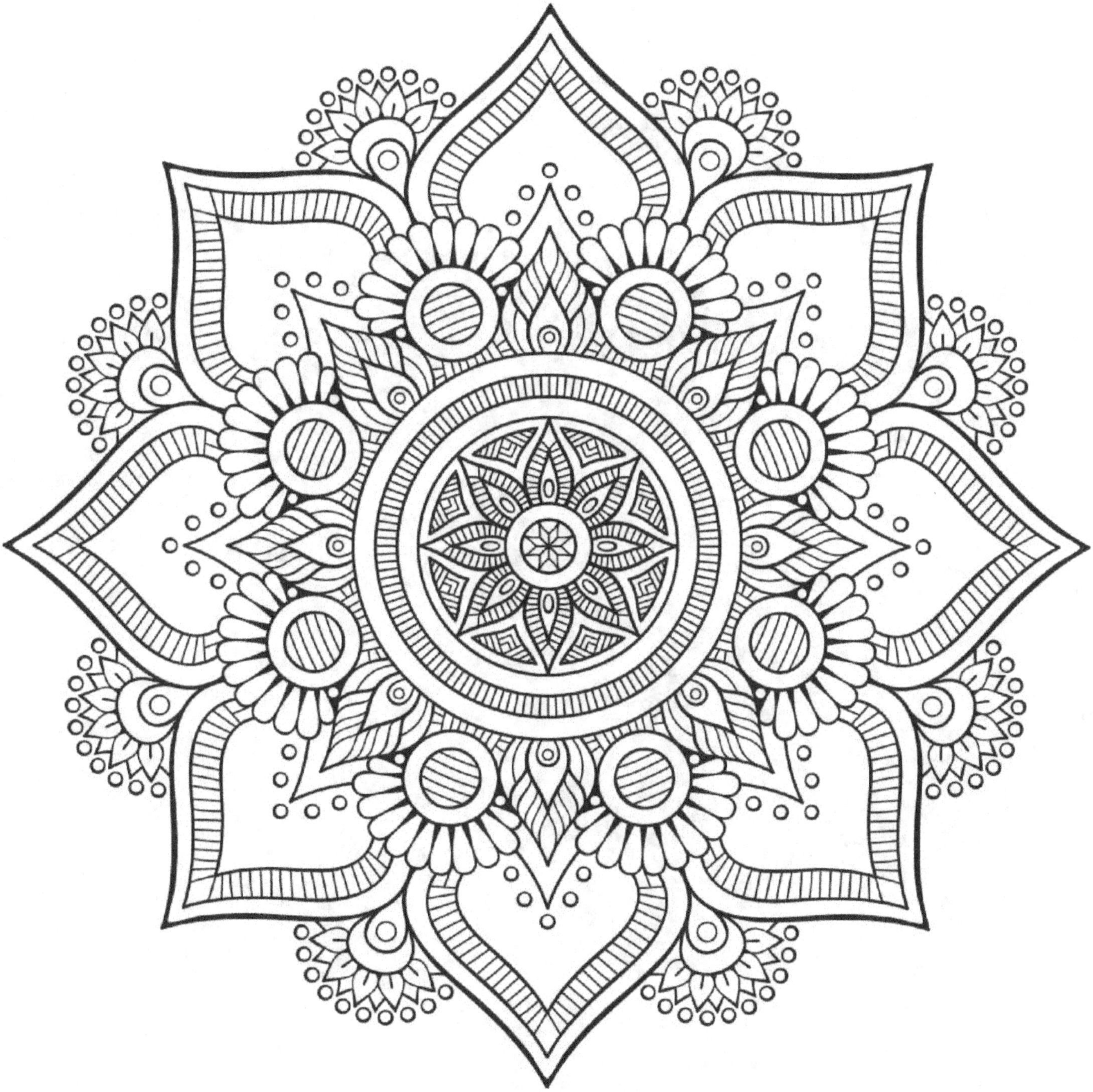

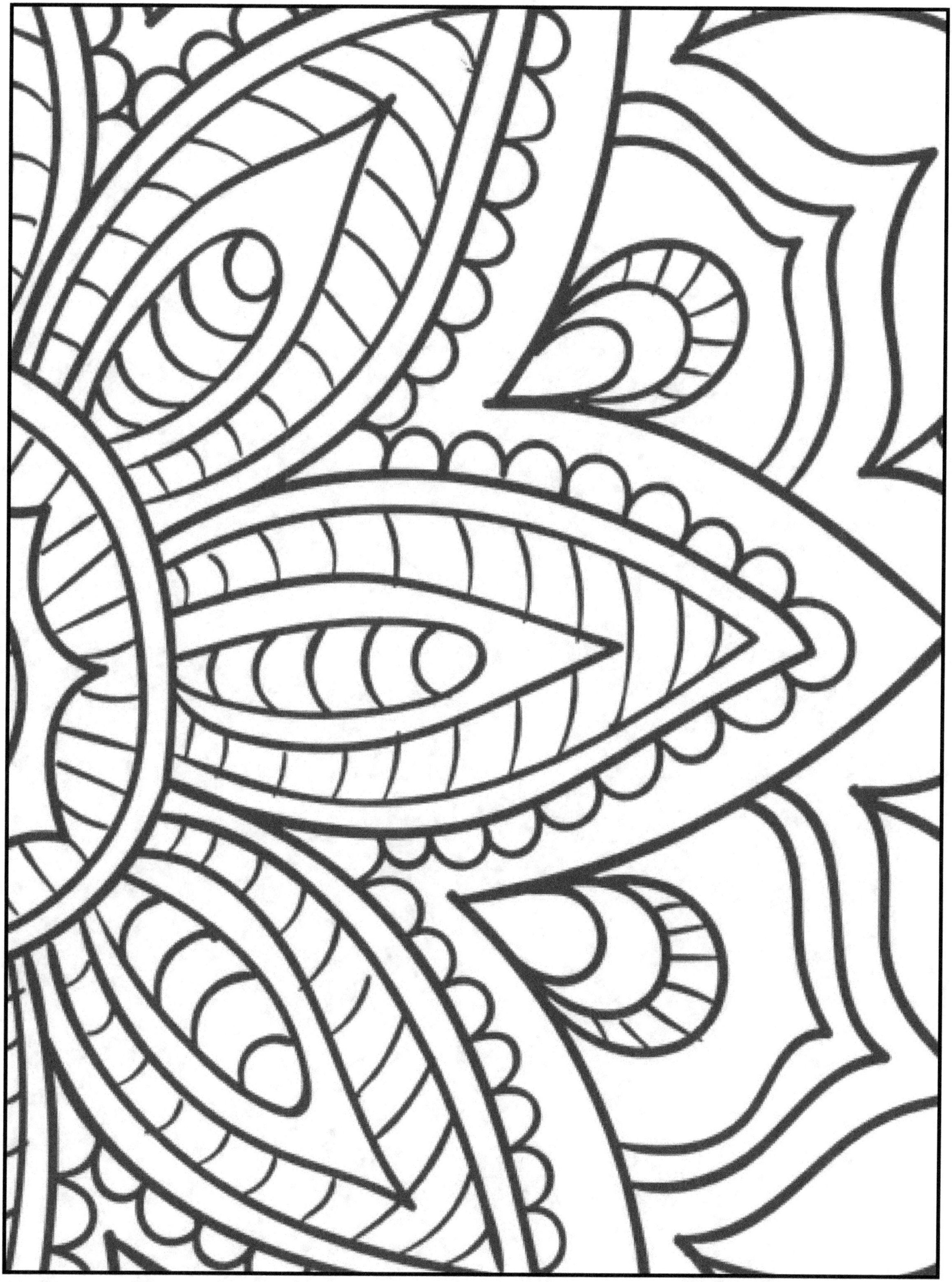

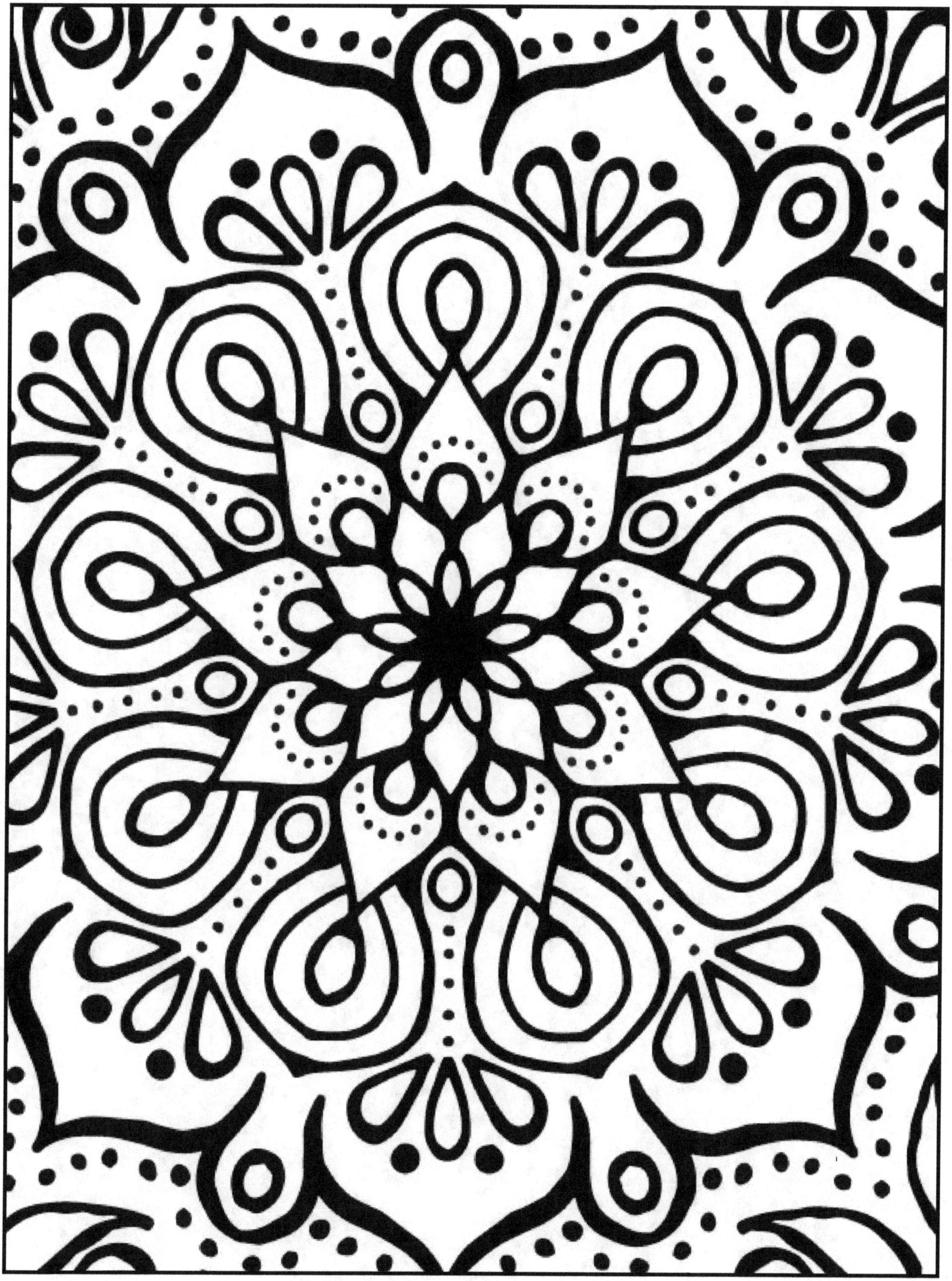

www.ingramcontent.com/pod-product-compliance
Lightning Source LLC
Chambersburg PA
CBHW081533220526
45467CB00010B/3161
* 9 7 9 8 6 9 6 3 3 7 8 7 6 *